After the Fires

NOZIPHO TSHABALALA

After *the* Fires

Unlocking the Power of Letting Go

Jonathan Ball Publishers
Johannesburg & Cape Town

Originally published in South Africa in 2025 by
JONATHAN BALL PUBLISHERS
A division of Media24 (Pty) Ltd
PO Box 33977
Jeppestown
2043

ISBN 978-1-77619-458-2
ebook ISBN 978-1-77619-459-9
Audiobook ISBN 978-1-77619-538-1

jonathanball.co.za
x.com/JonathanBallPub
facebook.com/JonathanBallPublishers

Cover by Melanie Kriel
Design and typesetting by Nazli Jacobs

Set in Palatino

In memory of my mother – for the gift of your fighting spirit and an unending well of self-belief.

For my father and my siblings – for the anchor your love is to me.

To my heartbeats, Rori and Tilo, without you, none of this.

Contents

ONE

Head-on Collision

'Nozi.'

'Answer your phone.'

'Ma is dead.'

I was seated before a two-thousand-strong audience, moderating a strong lineup of panellists. The stakes were higher than the normal studio-based conversation. We were broadcasting live into forty-eight African countries and there were eight million people watching in that moment.

The producer in my ear gave me a 30-second countdown to the advertisements. I steered us successfully to the break, quickly pulled my phone from beneath my bum to find my sister's three successive text messages. They were like fists to my throat.

Three days before, I was in a different province, basking in the heat of Limpopo, eating *tchotlo* and drinking *gemmer*. Rori and I loved road trips, so when a long weekend with an invitation to attend a tombstone unveiling ceremony in Limpopo came up, we immediately said yes. I tried to escape the heat and found a sliver of shade under the white tent where the formal speeches were taking place. We were giggling at the uncle who'd captivated the audience in his inebriated state, insisting on recounting memories of the deceased in a version of English that few of us could understand.

My phone rang. It was my Baba. He could wait. I would call after the speeches were done. The phone rang again. Baba wouldn't call twice unless something was wrong, so I stepped out of the shade of the tent and away from the crowd.

'Umawakho uwile.'

Baba spoke in uncharacteristically short and staccato sentences. My mother had collapsed, he told me, and he didn't know what to do. Could I come home? I made my way back to the tent, dazed, sat down next to Rori and stared ahead. The uncle was still speaking, sniggers continuing to ripple through the crowd. Rori turned to me so we could share a laugh but he saw that my face had turned to stone. He took my hand, got me to stand and led me away from the tent.

I can recall the 20-second conversation with my father, but the rest is a blur. I remember getting into the car but I don't remember the nine-hour drive from Mahwelereng in Limpopo to Lincoln Meade in Pietermaritzburg. I am sure that I must have made calls on the way to establish which hospital my mother was in.

I flew through the entrance at Northdale Hospital, navigating the maze that made up the labyrinth of the public health facility. With little signage, I stopped a nurse in the passageway to get the directions I needed. I rushed onwards.

It was visible that she'd had a stroke: the left side of my mother's face was sagging, her speech was slurred, her eyes were darting wildly in what appeared to be confusion and fear. More worryingly, my father told me that Ma had not yet received any medical care since having arrived almost ten hours earlier.

Why was she in a public hospital? We'd had the medical aid conversation only a few months earlier. My mom had called wanting to understand the difference between medical aid and a hospital plan and very proudly announced that she could now, as a teacher, afford to put herself and my father on a comprehensive plan. We never spoke of it again and I hadn't followed up. But I couldn't focus on that now. I made frantic calls to friends who were doctors. Everyone was gentle with me and relentless in getting my mother the help she needed. We managed to get a doctor to attend to her while we awaited an ambulance that would transfer her to a private hospital.

The siren of the ambulance and the wheels of the stretcher bed making its way toward us was all that I needed. I started to breathe again. I'd saved the day. True to the dichotomy of the South African health system, the private hospital had a team of doctors waiting to receive and attend to her.

When we were finally able to see Ma, the news was better than expected. The neurosurgeon confirmed the stroke but said my mother was showing all the signs of being able to recover without surgical intervention. Ma was strong and was clearly fighting to stay with us.

By the next day my mother's eyes were still and while her speech was still slurred, she pointed to her water when she wanted to drink and was showing signs of coming back to us. Even in this moment of frailty and physical weakness, I could see and feel my mother's fight. We didn't need words to communicate. Her work was not yet done. I knew it and she knew it. In the silence of the ward, punctuated only by the incessant beeps of the machines and murmured prayers of families around their own loved ones, our silent conversation was loud.

Rori and I were at the hospital at every possible visiting hour. My mother would need physiotherapy to fully regain the use of her body, and we were encouraged by the report that indicated that she wanted to write. Although the writing was illegible, it was a sign that she had not completely lost her language capabilities. If she could write, she could still speak, we were told. We had teased her incessantly over the years for her short temper and quickness to shout. With her capability for speech looking strong, we joked that we would not be spared her sharp tongue once she recovered!

Meanwhile, an hour's drive from the hospital, the *Essence Festival* – the largest African American culture and music event – was making its comeback to Durban, South Africa. The CNBC Africa team that was despatched to capture and broadcast the massive cultural event had been assembled and I'd been chosen to be one of the anchors to moderate the live panel discussion between Durban's political leadership and some of the international guests. I must have called my boss during the nine-hour drive from Mahwelereng to Lincoln Meade, cutting through provinces, to tell her what was happening and that I'd need to take some time to be with my family. But I soon realised that I needed to convince her that I wanted my place back on the team. I'd spent almost every waking moment during the past 72-hours either at the hospital or at home waiting to go back to the hospital.

'Bronwyn, I need this. I'm less than an hour away from the hospital. I need a distraction to keep me sane.'

The plan was simple. I was going to take a few hours to myself. I'd moderate on one of the biggest stages of my career, then I'd go back to my mother's bedside and figure out how to help her regain control over her life, and for me to recover my sense of self. The broadcast was in the morning, so I decided to book a hotel in Durban for the night so that I'd be close to the team at the 5 am call time. Rori would spend the night with me and then fly to Johannesburg as I joined the team for the day's production. Life wasn't great, but at least I was back in control.

We settled into the hotel for the night and for the first time talked about the bullet my family had just dodged. With slightly clearer heads and calmer hearts we lamented the poor service in the public hospital and shared our gratitude for the friends who had come through and helped us move Ma into a private facility where we felt death could be managed, and even averted. I checked in with my father. Things were as good as they could be. He'd just come back from the hospital and Ma was resting. I could now settle in for the night and wrap my head around the work I was to do in the morning.

My phone rang from my mother's number. It couldn't be! I felt a shaking sensation rising up in my body. I could barely hold the phone steady enough to answer. Questions chased each other around in my head. Could it be her calling? Was it someone else using her phone? Why would the nurses and doctors use a patient's phone? Was that even ethical?

'Answer it, love,' Rori encouraged.

Ma's voice slurred and stammered over the line. It was incoherent but it was her. She was speaking!

'M..u.sa ukuth..uka. Ngi..ngi..cela u..u..ngith..engele i-airtime. Ubu..ya ni..ni?'

It took her almost five minutes to deliver her reassurance, to ask me to buy her airtime, and to ask when I was coming back. The tears came then, flowing hot with relief, cleansing my body of exhaustion and my mind from the crippling fear of losing her. Everything was fine. Ma was back. I hadn't realised that in trying to survive the moment, I had coiled into myself. I was brittle with a fear that was masked as resilience and the belief that all *must* be well.

The next morning, I woke up feeling lighter and I as I took my seat on the stage I felt grounded and secure for the first time in days. The coil had begun to unfurl. More than anything, I couldn't wait to drive back to Pietermaritzburg to converse with my mother face-to-face. I could already imagine how we'd probably be teasing her for years to come about how much she'd scared us. My mother was a fighter; this was just another battle, one she'd just conquered.

The energy of two thousand people pulsating in the Durban International Convention Centre came at me like a wave hitting the stage. I loved the feeling! And it felt good to have something I could once again control. I was meticulous in my questioning, with each provocation flowing from one issue to the next as I weaved and threaded the conversation for my panellists. I was listening with my whole body, leaning into the silences and surfacing the insights. Moderating was what I imagined conducting an orchestra might feel like, bringing the right instrument into the symphony at the right time and blending all of these contributions into a magical rendition.

'Thirty seconds to ad break, Nozi.'

That was the moment I took a quick glance at my phone.

'Ma is dead.'

*   *   *

I was lost in an abyss of grief for a long time after my mother passed away.

As I watched my mother's body being lowered into the ground, I knew that everything I had thought to be true of the world was vanishing with the dust that was rising and falling on her casket. For the first time in my life, I was truly, utterly, lost.

With the help of prayer, therapy and some courageous conversations with myself and others, when I started to come out of the dark place that I'd sunk into, I could ask myself whether this was my personal head-on collision. Now that I had come face-to-face with my need for control, would I be able, in this shattering encounter, to release myself from living within the constricting lines of control? Was I ready to open the door to all the fears I had neatly managed and packed away? This was not a personal confrontation I was ready for; rather, it was one that had been patiently waiting for me.

I began a new conversation with myself about what control was and what it represented in my life. Part of this reflection forced me to acknowledge how control had served me well in many aspects of my life. Without the discipline I had exerted over almost everything in my life up till that point, I might not have made it to tell this story. Indeed, I think that being in control has saved my life. I watched my parents control everything that they could, to push me out of the pit of poverty our family was in. I learned that if I minimised risk and kept the playing field tight and well managed I'd make it out okay. The world was not my oyster. The world was a series of miniscule gaps of opportunity that could not, must not, be squandered. Creativity and curiosity were the preserve of those who had safety nets and wells of second chances.

It has been a seven-year journey of meeting myself anew since then. Kicking and screaming, I came to realise that the thing that served me most – *control* – was the thing that also threatened to hold me back, keeping me from a fulfilled life. I'm only now understanding that what got me *here might be the*

very thing that holds me here, keeping me from reaching 'there'.
To borrow from the words of the Reverend Victoria Safford
in her poem, *The Gates of Hope,* my 'history has been meeting
my hope at the gates of possibility for some time now'. When
my past and my future collided, I had a choice: to double
down and try to reclaim control over everything in my life,
or to get comfortable with relinquishing control and unlocking the power of letting go.

TWO

Before the Fires

Before the fires and the killings, I used to watch my father with a Rothmans cigarette in his mouth, the soft royal blue and white box in his shirt or trouser pocket, the corner open. There was the dance of smoke swirling that I'd try to reach from my position, perched on his knee. I ate chicken feet dipped in gravy and *uphuthu* with my hands from a yellow enamel bowl on the floor. I rode a red tricycle that whooshed down a dirt pathway lined with yellow flowers that stopped at a wire gate at the bottom of the garden. There was a pit latrine that I wasn't allowed to go inside of, because of the fear that I might fall in bum-first. Instead, I had to learn how to squat in the grass beside it, and to my irritation I'd stand up with a wet bottom on dewy mornings. Then the fires and the killings came into the yellow garden and torched down our home.

I was born into the clutches of political warfare. In the late 1980s leading to the early 90s, the province of Natal, now

KwaZulu-Natal (KZN), was engulfed in violent conflict as the African National Congress, the Inkatha Freedom Party, and the United Democratic Front fought for power and control of the KwaZulu homeland. As South Africa was working through the pains of transitioning from apartheid to a democratic state, KZN was being ravaged by violence akin to a civil war.

Another of my earliest childhood memories is clinging to my father's back, my mother beside him, as we fled the flames of our home that had just been petrol-bombed. I have snatches of disconnected memories of that time but my parents have filled in the gaps to help me understand myself in the context of the province in which I was born and the country I call home. After all, we are the sum total of all the places we've been. Just like a river that leaves its source, can travel through rugged landscapes, flow through valleys and canyons cutting through layers of rock and soil and rushing on towards waterfalls and rapids, we too are made up of all the places we've been and of all the people we've had to become on our way to where we finally find ourselves. The river might meander through lush forests, becoming a drinking place for wildlife and sustenance for banks lined with trees, it can trickle slowly towards farmlands, joining irrigation systems that produce crops and sustain flocks. That very same river may make its way into the belly of a city, serving as a source of recreation and transportation. We have moments that may feel as if we are meandering along and trickling very slowly towards our dreams.

All the experiences that we collect along our journey make

us who we are and eventually line up to fulfil the purpose for which we were born. The source of my river is in the heart of the mid-80s political conflict in KZN. My river moved in ebbs and flows, forcing my parents to flee to save our lives – my life, in particular. They made what I know must have been an achingly difficult decision to temporarily give me away so as to secure my safety while the country was securing its democracy.

*   *   *

From Edendale Hospital in Pietermaritzburg where I was born – now renamed Harry Gwala Regional Hospital (a leading teaching hospital) after the apartheid struggle icon – my story flows.

Like every black person I knew, I grew up calling Edendale *Eyideni* and I knew that this was where people went to die. My grandmother had passed away there, so had two of my cousins, as well as countless aunts and uncles. One of my mother's love languages was showing up to *Eyideni* with a bunch of bananas and *amahewu* for whomever was ill. When I saw this combination in her handbag, I knew that someone had been admitted to *Eyideni* and was about to die.

I made it out alive, leaving *Eyideni* wrapped in my mother's arms, a few days after 15 March 1984. I was named Nozipho Bridget Mbanjwa. Apparently, I was not the cutest of babies. My mother loved to tell the story of how I looked like a boy with a big head and skinny limbs and that she was forced to pierce my ears early so that I would be identified as a girl.

Nozipho means woman of multiple talents, or a woman of gifts, in the Nguni languages. I'm told my mother broke tradition to name me instead of giving her mother or her mother-in-law that privilege. My father says I was also given the name Bridget because he loved Aretha Franklin's rendition of *Bridge over Troubled Waters* and that he'd hoped that I would become this to my family. I think the fact that the apartheid state expected every child to have a registered Christian English name as they entered the schooling system was probably an even bigger reason for me to have received the English name.

From *Eyideni* the river ran to *eMaqongqo*. English-speaking people in KZN referred to this place as Table Mountain, so you can imagine my confusion when I learnt that this was the name of a very prominent landmark in an entirely different province, a good 18 hours' drive away. Still, *eMaqongqo* was our Table Mountain. But I have not retained many childhood memories of the place, something which my therapist attributes to the magnitude of the violence that I survived there.

My river meandered from the security we thought we had in *eMaqongqo* into the thickness of a forest, forced to hide from the violence. My father managed to bundle us into our white VW Passat to drive us away from the flames and the main roads as deep into the forest as the car could go. For some weeks, my mother and I stayed hidden in the car while my father went to look for food. When he returned, we'd share whatever he'd found or managed to buy. If it required cooking, my mother brought out the paraffin primus stove from the boot, wedged it between the front and back doors of the car to protect the flame from the wind, and prepared whatever meal she could. After a few weeks, with the frontier of the fighting coming ever closer, my parents made the decision to save my life by finding me a place of refuge while they fled as refugees. We were not struggle heroes, we were people caught in the crossfire between the ANC, IFP and the UDF.

Sources differ on the exact number of people who died during that period, though a consistent trend of approximately 100 deaths per month from 1989 until 1993 has emerged. In addition, almost half a million families were displaced.

While my parents remained on the run, I was hiding in plain sight. I was light-skinned enough to pass off as coloured, and with colourism in my corner and braids in my hair to hide its true texture, my parents took me to a daycare centre in a nearby coloured community that was harbouring children of parents fleeing the violence. I don't know what was promised, or how, if any, payment was made. What I do know is that when I arrived at the daycare centre my name became Bridget Anderson, and I was told that if anyone asked about my parents I was to point to Mr and Mrs Anderson. I can't imagine the risk that the Anderson family must have taken in passing me off as one of their own children.

Like a picture taken in portrait mode, the memories of my arrival and stay with the Andersons, who ran the daycare centre, are hazy, but a few things stand out brightly: there was a big gate that faced the main road. All the children whose parents picked them up at the end of the day would line up just inside the gate with school bags on shoulders, waiting for cars and *oMalume* in mini-bus taxis to take them home. I was part of the group that never went home. Inside the big gate in one corner was our jungle gym where limbs and imaginations stretched in the joy of play. In my young mind, the Andersons' home was huge. We had a classroom where we sang songs and recited numbers, and an open area where we had meals. Years later I would drive past this building and realise that it was just two four-bedroomed structures that had been converted into a daycare centre.

Often, when it was dark outside, my parents would arrive and speak to me in the language that I knew. On those nights, we'd gather together the small white mats with cartoon characters that the children used during the day for our naps and piece them together to form one large sleeping puzzle mat. I'd tell my parents about all the funny English words that I'd heard that day. Those were the best nights! By morning they'd be gone, and I'd wait patiently for the next time. I don't know how the Andersons and my parents managed to keep my mouth shut about these visits, but I realised later that significant risk was being managed on our behalf. I don't know exactly how long I stayed at the Andersons, but I recall that the day my parents fetched me, I was told that I was going to start 'big school' soon and that I would now live with my parents.

As a mother today, I can't imagine what it must have been like for my parents to give me up to be raised elsewhere:

I keep catching myself in moments as I try to control all the conditions of the environment in which my son is raised, from the food that he eats to the words that are spoken to, and about, him. I can appreciate that in my parents' context the alternative was death. They would only relinquish control under threat of death – for everything else, we would have to manage.

This moment would become a blueprint for me. Control was everything; you only gave it up when all other options had been exhausted.

My parents and I moved into a caravan, parked in the front yard of a family in a nearby township called Glenwood. I later learnt that there was a rental arrangement with the owners of the caravan – a small capsule-like container with just enough space for a single bed for the three of us, our clothes neatly packed in a suitcase underneath the bed. There was a single rectangular cabinet in which to keep our food, on top of which was a two-plate stove for all the meals my mother prepared. There were strict instructions to never go and bother the people in the big house, and to only ever stay in the caravan unless otherwise instructed. My mother worked in the main house doing the family's laundry, ironing and other chores, as she did for a few families in the street on alternate days.

My river had trickled to this new place in which I would be reminded that my first name was Nozipho. This was what I answered to in the caravan while Bridget was reserved for school. In 1990, the South African education system still required that black learners have English Christian names, and so my second name was used instead of my first. My parents felt it important to remind me, and to constantly reinforce, that I was not actually an Anderson. Now that I had left the place of safety, I was a Mbanjwa again, and this was the surname I had to remember going forward. More importantly, I needed to be mindful to speak isiZulu at home and English at school. Of course, from time to time, in the presence of aunts, uncles and cousins, I needed to show everyone that I could speak English, and with an accent to boot!

I settled into this new duplicity just like a child learns multiple languages: with ease. Nozipho at home, Bridget at school. But the complications were not done with. My father had found employment in a nearby shoe factory, hand-stitching moccasins. This job would be a force multiplier in our family and my river would push forward towards new opportunities.

My father was hired by a Mr Roberts, whom I would come to know as a kind and generous man. His generosity would change the trajectory of my life. Mr Roberts owned a factory called Sirilli Shoes and he took an interest in our whole family. The factory was next to Johnnie's, a tavern that never seemed to be without patrons, irrespective of the time of day. Sirilli Shoes and Johnnies were at the entrance to Eastwood, a neighbouring coloured township. It's not lost on me that the physical location of the tavern, as the first thing you encountered in this township, was more than a landmark but a metaphor for the ever-present role of alcohol in township life. My mother supplemented my father's salary from Sirilli

Shoes by setting up a table outside the factory and selling food and fruit to the workers during their breaks. With my father's better salary and my mother's vending table, we moved out of the caravan and into a peach-painted council house with white trim that stood on Eastwood's Kingklip Road.

I don't know how we got allocated a council house in a community designated as 'for coloured people'. The Group Areas Act of 1950 had come into full force by 1960, and the townships of Eastwood, Woodlands and Glenwood had been earmarked for coloured people only. Many families had been forcefully removed from areas like Pentrich and Upper and Central Church Street as these became zoned for white people. Like all forced removals, it was a painful time for coloured families who had to leave homes, livelihoods and decades of memories behind. More horrifically, many families were separated when some members – more white-looking than coloured – reclassified as white, moving to different neighbourhoods to live entirely distinct lives from their families. While being relocated to these poorer parts of Pietermaritzburg was undoubtedly traumatic, a strong sense of community built up over time, and coloured people felt that they had a place of their own in a racially segregated South Africa. It was better to be coloured than black, but best – if at all possible – to be white.

This sense of community, however, also translated into a resistance to any black families trying to establish homes in coloured communities. But there we were, in a narrow structure that had three tiny bedrooms upstairs, one bathroom and a lounge and a kitchen downstairs. When I think about that house today, I realise that the floor size of the entire house was just the size of my kitchen today. The vertical structure was a genius move by the council, as more units could be built without taking up more square metrage, and they could simply be separated by painting them different colours. Our house was in the first row of council houses, and a stone's throw away from Eastwood Secondary School. We were furthest away from 'Beverley Hills', which was where the most affluent people lived, in homes that they'd built themselves and now owned.

I made friends easily. My stay with the Andersons had prepared me, even though I'd been so young, to move fluidly between identities and spaces. The coloured accent was second nature to me and on the hopscotch streets my friend nicknamed me Bree, short for Bridget. I learnt that every elderly woman was aunty and every man was uncle. We bought and sucked on condensed milk at one house, bright red toffee apples at another and never missed flavoured ice blocks at ten cents apiece.

We were also close to Thembalihle, a squatter camp that seemed to have arisen overnight and was growing rapidly as black families continuously poured in, still fleeing the hotspots of violence in different parts of the city. To our extended family, who could only dream of such opulence, we'd made it. We lived in a double-storeyed house in a coloured community, and that was way more than they had.

While my parents moved with hesitant steps in this new community that resisted the entry of black people, I moved with more confidence at school. Raisethorpe Primary School – now known as Forest Hill Primary – was racially integrated for black and coloured learners. The school had a bus that would pick us up and drop us off at the various stops in Eastwood, Woodlands or Glenwood. I was among the gaggle of maroon tunics, white shirts and grey shorts on the bus to and from school. In the afternoons, I would get off at Sirilli's and go to the factory to wait for my father to knock off before walking home together. I loved school! My competitive spirit was nurtured, and every term came with the much-anticipated report card that would earn me praise at home and give my parents bragging rights until the next term started. I only ever wanted to come first, but on several occasions had to settle for second or third.

I learnt early that doing well at school made my parents proud and set me, and them, apart from the 'the rest'. The harder I worked on my reading, writing and counting, the more adults looked to me as a special child. At some point I also cracked the code that the correct answer to 'what do you want to be when you grow up' was: 'a doctor'. My parents would beam with pride and it would confirm for all those within earshot that I was smart and destined for a big and very important job.

Mrs Abrahams was my first teacher. She was slim and wore the most beautiful colourful dresses. She wore her curly ginger hair in a short pixie cut and I thought she was perfect. She was, however, liberal with her stick and would let us have it for making a noise or being late. This is where I first learnt crippling compliance: to avoid a beating, I needed to be as close to perfect as possible.

My next teacher taught me confidence. She praised my reading ability, which fuelled my love for reading. She encouraged me to sign up for a library card at the Eastwood Library. It was a gift that my mother and I bonded over. On Saturday mornings we would walk to the library and I'd pick up two or more copies of *Sweet Valley High*, which narrated the escapades of identical twins, Jessica and Elizabeth Wakefield. My mother would get her dose of Mills & Boon novels with the sultry covers. I don't think she realised how advanced I'd become in my reading and that my offer to return her books was only because I'd get to scan a few pages on the way. I lost myself in the descriptive language of lovemaking and all the sexual and sensual things, best described in a Mills & Boon.

After school, while waiting for my father at Sirilli's, Mr Roberts would invite me into his office to do my homework. He'd check it too and help if he saw that I was struggling. We grew very close. With a balding head and wrinkly skin, he felt like a grandfather and doted on me like one. I was a scrawny 7-year-old sitting in the boss's office practising my sums, spelling and handwriting while my father's calloused hands worked heavy machinery on the factory floor. From time to time Mr Roberts' children would come by the factory to visit their father. They were much older than I was, and they treated me like their parent's *laat lammetjie*. They spoilt me with books, dolls and sweets at every visit. The trips to the factory became home visits, and then sleepovers at their house. I was finding my place in the new South Africa: a black child in a coloured community who would have the doors to democracy fully swung open by a white family.

In 1994, the year I turned 10 years old, Mr Roberts completed an application on my behalf and put up the funds for me to go to a school previously reserved for white children only. Scottsville Primary had opened its doors to black learners three years earlier. I arrived to start my Grade 4 year in Mrs Chapman's class. There were just two learners who were not white in the class, myself and an Indian boy, Viresh, who became my biggest competition academically. Mrs Chapman encouraged all of us and was attentive and present for all her learners. At one point she left to have a baby and was back in the classroom by the following week! In Mrs Chapman's class, and on the playground, I needed to learn to be white – and to do so fast. I was already different with the thin shoulder-length braids that my mother had painstakingly plaited herself over the course of a full day the weekend before school had started. My thick coloured accent drew giggles from the other learners in class, and I knew that it had to change. I needed to learn to pronounce my words with a softer, more rounded delivery, *less coloured, more white*. My lunchbox changed from my mother's delicious *phuthu* and cabbage leftovers to cheese sandwiches with a side of heavily diluted Oros. I convinced my mother that the Waltons stationery list we received at school was a non-negotiable, and that the neon-coloured space-case was as important as the uniform itself – which it was!

I became a master of moving between different cultural contexts and knowing how far to go in search of belonging without losing sight of my own feet. I spoke English with a white accent at school, English with a coloured accent with my friends in the streets of Eastwood, and isiZulu in my own voice at home. This was my world, characterised by a fluidity of identity shifts as the moment demanded. I assimilated when I needed to, performed the cultures of others when required and upheld my own language and sense of self when I could. I was the resident translator in the family. Anyone who needed to complete application forms or a motivation letter for a job application, or to write a letter of complaint would turn to me. For my family, I was learning what it really meant to become a bridge over troubled waters and for myself I was learning what control looked like in the adult world.

My river flowed under more bridges and into Pietermaritz-burg Girls' High School, or GHS, as we called it. It was an easy decision for me, but I believe it must have been a very difficult one for my parents because in my final year at Scotts-ville, Mr Roberts passed away. The person who had not only shown me kindness and warmth but who had also funded my primary schooling, was no longer there to do so. All my friends were going to GHS, so my feelings were on the line. I also think that my parents didn't want the shame of my 'going back' to a coloured school and the perception of re-gression. More importantly, I would later realise that, in allowing me to go to GHS, my sisters would have to go to Eastwood Secondary School just up the road from our house. The decision to give me the best possible chance came with a corollary: my sisters could only get what was left, what was affordable, planting resentment between me and my siblings as they struggled with the question of 'why her, and why not me?'

As for Mr Roberts, I had not known that he was waging a battle for his life against stomach cancer. When he passed away, his family shared two gifts that he'd left for me. The first was a picture of the two of us at his home which must have been taken at one of my many sleepovers. I was wearing one of his big T-shirts and I was kneeling on the couch behind him as he sat on the floor in front of me. In my hand was a wide-toothed comb that I was running through his wisps of hair. Neither of us was looking at the camera. I was fully focused on the moment, and he seemed to know that it was almost gone. The second gift was a frame with my name written in his neat handwriting at the back. It was a copy of Mary Stevenson's poem, *Footprints in the Sand*.

My mother framed the picture and hung it alongside the poem, also framed, in our lounge. Of course, these were designed to be a conversation starter for everyone who walked into the house.
    'Ubani lo mlungu?'
    'Is that Nozi?'
    For me, too, even at my young age, they elicited quiet reflection.

With the passing of Mr Roberts came the closure of Sirilli Shoes. My father was without a job, and our only income was from my mother's vending table, which was now set up outside the school gates of Eastwood Secondary School. As the learners arrived in the morning and left in the afternoon, they'd hopefully be enticed by my mother's display of fresh fruit, chips and cigarettes, the last of these hidden from the view of the teachers.

It was not enough. We needed more money to keep me at GHS and the entire family afloat. To add to this, the family had expanded over time as different cousins came to stay with us. We might have struggled, but in comparison to where my cousins were coming from, we were an often sought-out safe haven. Over the course of my childhood, my parents were always raising between three and eight children in our three-bedroomed house.

I don't know how, but my parents soon bought an Albany trailer-container. Yes, one of those containers pulled by a truck and from which bread is delivered to homes and spaza shops in townships across the country. One day a tow truck simply pulled into our backyard and dumped the container between the gate and the road. The next day we opened a telephone centre. This was in the days before internet cafés in the townships and the Albany container became a place for the community to make phone calls. The small vending table my mother had manned was replaced with shelving at the back of the container, and we now had a spaza-slash-telephone centre. Business was booming. Very few people had their own cell phones and the foot traffic from our customers in Eastwood and the neighbouring squatter camp, eThembalihle, made for good business. We all pitched in. While my mother ran the enterprise, my father took care of buying and keeping track of the stock of fresh produce and other perishables. Before school, we helped with frying *amagwinya*, and after school we had to separate the long bags of wholesale chips into micro packages of 50 cents each. Because I took taxis to school, I was often tasked with buying the wholesale bags of chips on my way home. It was always a grounding experience, a firm reminder that no matter how fancy the school I had just come from was, my family was not fancy. We were ordinary people, using whatever was at our disposal and making it work. In my school uniform and backpack, I would tuck each wholesale bag like a soft log under each armpit, cheese flavour on one side, chilli on the other, backpack on my back, and make for the taxi.

I arrived at GHS in 1998 in an oversized green dress that I was assured I'd grow into, and brown Toughees lace-ups. GHS was my river coming into a valley of abundance. I joined a large group of just over one hundred girls whom I'd journey with for the next five years.

South African classrooms were beginning to reflect the mosaic of the country. We were a diverse group: those 'who had' were paired with those 'who didn't have'; there were surnames that carried political weight and surnames which put some on the wrong side of history. Many girls stayed within the boarding school system and had three solid meals and a warm bed, while others awoke at dawn in overcrowded beds or on the floor, and needed multiple taxis to get to the classroom. But once we stepped into the grounds of GHS, the green uniform was our equaliser.

At GHS, I found a school trying to transform in response to the larger democratic project in the country. GHS had been started from the home of Peter and Mary Davis in 1920. I imagine that the conversation between the couple could not have been an easy one. They lived in Morningside, a Victorian-style mansion, that they sold to the Natal Education Department for the establishment of Pietermaritzburg Girls High School. Educating girls in that era could not have been an easy decision or investment to make. Women in South Africa didn't even have the right to vote in 1920 and when that right finally came to South Africa in 1930, only white women were considered eligible. Before 1920, boys' education was considered an important investment into society and Pietermaritzburg High School, later renamed Maritzburg College, was a boys-only school opened as early as 1863, while girls' education was largely limited to primary education, with only a few schools like Model Primary School (later to become Russel High School in 1941) and Longmarket School for Girls being established.

When Ms Norma Burns, the first principal at GHS, was invited to take up the post by the Natal Education Department, she first had to present a case to prove that there was sufficient societal interest, demand and viability for an all girls high school in Pietermaritzburg.

The school's motto was 'cheerfulness with industry', and an ethos of industriousness certainly seeped through the red brick corridors and into everything the school offered. I was encouraged to do whatever I had an interest in: I played soccer, I was part of the debating team, I joined the Representative Council of Learners (RCL), I played basketball and netball. Anything and everything. There was one rider, though: the buck stopped at anything that required expensive gear. When I came home with an interest in trying out for the rowing team, my father had to draw the line.

'Nozi ufuna is'kebe?'

It was not just the school's offering that made GHS such an important part of my life; it was also the girls and the teachers. I learnt from the girls who came from political families. At school, they transmitted stories from their dinner tables and in these conversations I would later find my own small acts of activism. With the exception of a few very close friends, everyone called me Bridget. It was not my first name, but the name I'd carried with me from my first encounter with school. In Grade 11, when I needed to complete my application for university, I claimed my birth name back in those two small blocks on the form . . .

Name: Nozipho
Surname: Mbanjwa

It was more than just a name; it was reclaiming what had been taken from me before I even knew I had it. I'm not sure this could have happened without the environment at GHS.

I also listened to the stories of white girls who'd come across from the Zimbabwean border. They were farmgirls whose families had lost farms as part of the land reform programme in Zimbabwe that had started in 1980 with the signing of the Lancaster Agreement. I sat with girls whose parents were trade union leaders, and those who came from homes carried on the salaries of teachers and nurses.

In the classroom we were encouraged to lead with our experiences and assured that every experience was valid. We debated even as we were learning how to be politically correct. We didn't always get it right. Like any environment with young girls finding themselves and their place in the world, it got ugly at times. There were occasional racial flare-ups, bullying and threats of 'after school is after school' when the moment called for it. At other times our teachers were visibly out of their depth. When isiZulu was introduced in the curriculum, our white biology teacher was assigned to teach the language to a class of black girls. That experiment didn't last. But slowly the teaching body evolved. We started to see black adults who were more than just cleaners and grounds-keepers. Our isiZulu teachers stood out in a sea of white around them. I can't imagine what it must have taken to balance the need for a teaching body that was diverse with a true reflection of the learners in the classroom against the fact that parents chose GHS because it had white teachers.

'*Ha! Ufunda nabelungu!*'

I had wonderful teachers throughout the five years, but none had more impact on me than Valerie Fowler. She was my English teacher and my netball and basketball coach. I think her role both in and outside of the classroom allowed her to see me, and other learners, more fully.

It's hard to capture Val's impact, but a distinct conversation stands out. She knew I was competitive. I liked to win – I still do, because winning means control. I tried out for many teams under her coaching. The year I turned 16, when netball season came about, I was bouncing on my toes, ready for the try-outs and for the under 16 A-team. I'd been in the A-team for the past two years and expected my place in this team too. The try-outs were tough. We were all coming into our bodies, girls were taller and faster. The sports field was an equaliser in many ways. Here, it didn't matter if you were an A-student in this or that. It didn't matter what type of home you came from or who your parents were. The only thing that mattered was whether your body and mind understood how to play the game, and if you could outpace and outmanoeuvre your opponent. There were only seven spots in the team and at least 30 girls looking to claim them.

I needed a strategy – another mechanism I would learn and adopt to help me stay in control. My height had already ruled me out of competing for the positions of goal shooter, goal attack, goalkeeper or goal defence. I wasn't tall but I was fast and aggressive. However, I couldn't sprint continuously for an hour across the attacking and defending thirds that make up most of the court. I lacked the stamina for centre – the endurance of the centre must carry the player in both attacking and defensive plays, a never-tiring Duracell battery. I wasn't it. But I could still compete for wing attack and wing defence.

I loved wing attack more than wing defence. A wing attacker plays with a lot more kinetic energy, moving to create space, making fast runs and outstepping the wing defence.

This made sense to me. My life was all about creating opportunity even in the most hopeless circumstances. I understood the world of staying ahead of whatever was designed to hold one back. The challenge I had was that the wing attack position was also being contested by someone who was visibly better than me. She was faster, played smarter and moved with a fluidity that I just couldn't muster. As for wing defence: a quick and agile player had to work to intercept the flow of the wing attack. The movement of the wing defence was a lot more strategic and measured, even while keeping up with the wing attack. My conclusion was that the only way to make the team would be to compete for wing defence. My strategy was to make the team on the wing defence card and then prove to Mrs Fowler, through substitute opportunities throughout the season, that I could play both attack and defence positions. In the try-outs I left everything on the field.

The team lists were always posted outside the sports office, and the announcement that the lists were up would come over the intercom just before break. Nobody bothered with food – we all ran to the sports office. I ran my finger over the A-team list, top-down and bottom-up. Where was my name? With the screams of joy and celebration raining down all around me, I turned to the B-team. There I was: wing defence. I hadn't made the A-team. In fact, I hadn't even been placed as a wing attack in what I considered to be a substantially weaker team. I stood for a while just looking at the wall, not really seeing the names. Slowly the girls left the sports office, the A-team girls high-fiving each other triumphantly. As

I stood alone, still staring at the wall, Miss Fowler came to stand beside me.

'Bridget, you decide how this story continues.'

It wasn't the pep talk or the pick-me-up one would expect, and it certainly wasn't what I wanted to hear. Still, in those few words, I got all the pick-me-up I needed. I was reminded that I could decide how to react to not making the team, and that I had control over my behaviour flowing from my feelings. I could sulk and show up poorly in the B-team, leave the squad altogether and come up with a story to make myself feel better. Or I could study the A-team, specifically the wing attack and the wing defence positions, to learn from those who were better than me.

Beyond the curriculum, Miss Fowler taught me about myself and who I was in the context of others. This was my experience with most of my teachers at GHS. While there were visible struggles that required them to find themselves in the new South Africa, for the most part, in my view, everyone was trying. And yet it was quite possible to walk the same corridors, sit in the same classrooms and be coached by the same teachers, and walk away with an entirely different experience.

In years since, I've become increasingly attuned to the voices of fellow old girls of GHS who've shared very different experiences of their time there. Their memories of GHS surfaced pain and hurt, suffered at the hands of racists and homophobes. I've often wondered whether I was so busy being grateful just to be there and preserving my place that I completely missed the very different experiences I've come to hear about. Or could it be that being so focused on what I *could control* didn't allow me to pay attention to, or to entertain, what I *could not control*? Perhaps I did see other students at the receiving end of racism, but I pushed this to my peripheral vision because I needed to decide which variables were working in my favour?

It felt like coming full circle when I returned to GHS decades later, retracing my own footprints in the sand, to work with the first male principal, Andrew Graaf, on institutionalised racism. While much had changed over the years, many things remained the same. Using GHS as an anchor, I worked with a small team of GHS staff to set up Conversation Clubs in surrounding schools. These clubs were run by the learners themselves and served as safe spaces for courageous conversations about what learners were confronted with in their everyday environment. It was important to me that I not become a fly-in and fly-out consultant, but that, instead, we build internal capacity to carry and sustain a culture of courage when it came to talking about hard things.

* * *

Likening my childhood to the movement of a river has helped me to appreciate every single experience I've had, including experiences that have been less than ideal. I was forced into living with and understanding people's differences before any child should have to. Developing fluency in different cultures was not something I could opt out of, and it has become a core part of my DNA that constitutes who I am today. As a child, I often found myself searching for belonging and quickly learning that I had to achieve this without losing sight of who I was, that it was quite possible to go to the edge – connect with others – even while I stood at the centre of who I believed I was. I could not have developed this muscle and capability if I didn't feel in control of who I needed to be, exercising it when needed. I learnt from my parents that I could put down an identity and assume an entirely different one, especially if my life depended on it. *I control who I am.* That lesson has stayed with me.

THREE

Blood Tears

It probably started when everyone descended on our home. One-year-old me could not have known what was about to happen. I'm able to imagine the day because I watched my sisters go through the rituals of *ukugcatshwa* – marking the faces of infants as an identifier of a specific surname or clan – on the day of their first birthday. Historically, this might have been done with sharp objects like a broken bottle that might easily pierce the skin, but over time more efficient tools like razor blades became more commonly used.

Our paternal great-grandmother, uKhokho, arrived first, and over a few days uncles and aunts made their way to our home too. Then, as the sun broke through the early morning, my great-grandmother called for a large plastic bowl, a *vas-kom*, small enough to be wedged between her thighs as she squatted on the floor, yet big enough to hold a wriggling toddler. I don't recall our family having a kraal, but I would imagine that had we had one, this ritual would have been

35

performed in the midst of the smell of cow dung and the bellowing of the family's cattle against the backdrop of rolling hills. Ours was a patchwork experience of practising Zulu cultures in coloured spaces, wedged into township life.

With my sisters it was performed on the front stoep of our home in Eastwood. Khokho's razor blade emerged from where it was tucked close to her breast and with quick, deft strokes she made cuts into my siblings' faces. One on the forehead and four on each cheek. Blood, tears. Apparently our uKhokho was adamant that the cuts needed to be small and not ruin our good looks and she was insistent that the cuts that my father and all his siblings had received not be repeated in our generation.

My sisters screamed and cried bitterly for my mother, like as I imagine I must have done too. A red, sandy substance, wrapped and tied in a piece of clear plastic, emerged from her other breast. She rubbed the substance into the cuts, eliciting even more screams and tears. I swore to myself that before I married anyone I'd first check if this was part of their cultural rituals because, if it was, they could count me out!

My mother stepped forward and scooped up the child from the *vaskom* that had collected the blood. I have no clue what happened to that blood but judging by how quickly it was whisked away by the uncles, I imagine it fulfilled yet another important function to mark the first year of our lives. While that was happening, my father shaved our heads and the hair was also collected by one of the uncles. The ritual then turned to the spilling of a different type of blood. There'd been a goat at each of my sister's *ukugcatshwa* ceremonies. It was slaughtered by the men, cooked by the women, and everyone would feast on it. The liver was the preserve of the elderly men in the family, while the women had their fair share of the intestines. The gates were opened and neighbours would file in, following the smell of the meat and partaking in the feast. The goat's skin was hung up to dry over a few days and Khokho stayed until it had completely dried. On the day she declared it was ready, it was cut and sewed to form *imbheleko*. Sturdy and rough, it was the perfect blanket with which to carry a baby on the back.

There were many cultural practices and rituals that made up the tapestry of my early childhood memories. I grew up with a dedicated place in the house where incense was burnt, and my father would approach the ancestors on our behalf, gently asking, and sometimes pleading, for whatever the family needed at a particular point. While I was being raised in this staunchly traditional Zulu family inside the house, I was also being raised in a very different reality outside the house.

The Eastwood suburb in Pietermaritzburg where I grew up was incredibly violent.

Flanked on one side by Glenwood and on the other by Woodlands, these three places comprised the city's coloured townships. It was also the three sites of war between the different coloured gangs. My family and I stayed in Eastwood for 17 years – these were formative years, from where I derive many of my core, hardwired memories. Despite the violence I saw and encountered, today I still fully identify as a person who is a proud product of a coloured community. I still often describe myself as 'black who grew up coloured'. There was a lot of beauty in the midst of the violence.

We were a community that loved music. We'd try to out-compete each other with who could blare their speakers the loudest from their home. The size of your sound system and the bass it could emit was the ultimate marker of cool. Sundays were for Tamia, Tevin Campbell and *Boys II Men*. On Friday nights, elderly neighbours sat outside on their stoeps while the young men and women would catch up over 750 ml quarts of beer on the street corner. R Kelly's *Bump and Grind* and TLC's *Waterfalls* would blend into each other as we walked up and down the street. Given that it was the end of the week, we'd also be allowed to play a little longer outside. This was the time to don Doc Martens and cheeky shorts, and we'd sing all the *Boom Shaka* songs we knew. Local mini bus taxis were part of this musical culture. They'd be spray painted in bright colours and branded with names like The Teddy Bear or Mr Lover-Lover. The owners would sometimes forgo the opportunity of earning the fare of four passengers by removing the back row seats and replacing these with massive speakers that would make the route to school or work a musical experience of note.

We loved looking good. Cleanliness was everything. We didn't need an occasion to be dressed in all white, finished off with a pair white Jack Purcell's or All Star takkies. Levi's were a must-have. Always clean, always tailored to perfection.

Style was everything. I got my first Levi's Jeans only when I turned 18. My mother was adamant that I could be coloured all I wanted but not on her pocket! She refused to buy me All Stars, so it was one of the first things I bought with my first salary. A childhood dream realised!

Boys and girls shared different ways to straighten one's hair: from the relaxers that, if not perfectly timed, could burn through to your scalp, to sleeping with rollers for the perfect curls in the morning, or a headwrap for the boys to wake up with the perfect tightly curled waves just like *K-Ci & JoJo*. Hair was a marker of sophistication and class: the straighter it was, the fancier you were. When we ran out of curse words in the middle of a fight as children, 'Your hair is kroes!' was the ultimate comeback and mic drop.

Two doors away from our house lived one of my closest childhood friends, Siyabonga: a common Zulu name for boys that means 'the family is thankful'. Because of his constant broad smile and his striking white teeth against his rather dark skin tone, we called him Smiler. Like me, Smiler was black but wore his coloured identity well. He was tall and loved to dance. If there was a new move, we all knew that Smiler would be the one to teach it to us. With his lanky limbs he made choreography look effortless. He introduced all of us to *Bone Thugs-N-Harmony* and taught us all the lyrics. Smiler and I grew up together from the age of eight, and he was probably only two years older than me. We went to Sunday school together, rehearsed Bible verses together, played hopscotch – heck, we took on each other in the 100-metre dash to the end of the road every now and then. With his long legs I never stood a chance but I would die trying. I would frequent Smiler's house because they sold bread and other small commodities that I was sent to buy as part of our own day-to-day living.

As we approached our teenage years, I have no doubt that my parents signalled to me that, as a teenage girl, a close friendship with a boy was considered inappropriate, and so Smiler and I slowly grew apart. I think that our natural curiosities as young teenagers also saw him gravitate towards the boy gangs in Eastwood while I increasingly spent more time indoors and behind our gates.

December was a notorious time for the boy gangs to avenge and revenge each other and what should have been a festive season often came with reports of young boys stabbing and shooting each other. Inevitably, deaths and funerals would follow. One December, Smiler had been involved in a fight and had been stabbed in the shoulder. I was mortified but quickly realised that he wore his stab wounds as a badge of honour. Topless, including on the rainy December days, he strutted up and down the street for all to see that he too had been stabbed.

My parents didn't want me to be exposed to any of this and so, increasingly, any friendships with the coloured teenagers became strained. I always felt that my parents were being unreasonable, though I saw the evidence for myself of boys nursing stab wounds and limbs wrapped up over Christmas and the new year.

In the year that I turned 16, Smiler must have been around

18, he was shot three times in the face and killed on site. According to those on the scene, he was attending a dancing competition and had been drinking with his friends. Unknowingly, he approached the girlfriend of one of the rival dance groups, which led to a confrontation. The girl's boyfriend shot him in the middle of the street, leaving his skull shattered. In the weeks that followed, those who told the story while hanging over garden hedges in their dressing gowns, or tightly squeezed in a taxi on the way to work, said that his grandmother had had to scoop up what remained of his skull – as if she could pick up the life that had been splattered against the tar and hold it once again against her bosom. They say that she waited for the police and mortuary officials for hours, never leaving Smiler's side, lest some of his body parts became trampled by the crowd that continued to play music and dance as if nothing had happened.

I share Smiler's story precisely because it wasn't special – stories of such a nature were no longer shocking in the community in which I was raised. In fact, it was the norm to have young boys killing each other, as it was the norm for young girls to fall pregnant at an early age, potentially having multiple children before they turned 20, while for those who made it through high school, the best outcome was often working in a factory not too far from our homes. Eastwood, Glenwood and Woodlands were all on the edges of industrial zones propped up by shoe factories, sunflower oil manufacturers and timber factories.

I do not attribute my luck to having avoided these stereotypes to my own knowledge, but rather to the strong controls my parents instituted to keep me away from the focal points of violence and early sexual encounters. Control kept me safe and alive. I have no other way of explaining why my life was spared when I was in the heart of the storm and could, at any given moment, have become collateral damage in one of the many small wars around us.

Smiler's death had a profound impact on me. It confronted me with this choice: was I going to end up in a coffin like he had or was I going to make it out of Eastwood? The fact that I had the opportunity to go to schools outside of Eastwood also meant that I already had a different perspective on life. At a young age I'd begun to understand that I didn't have to follow the path I'd seen my peers taking.

Outside of our gate, danger always lurked. As we grew into our teens, we were discouraged from making friends and playing in the street. Playing outdoors was slowly reined in as my body filled out. By the time I got to high school, I knew people in our street, but didn't really know anyone well. I was isolated from friends I'd grown up with, and staying indoors was considered a virtue. My parents would proudly point out to visitors that their daughters would not be found in the streets and only walked the path from school to home. The random weekly stabbings and shootings only justified their stance and would often be shared as a reminder that remaining isolated was a safety measure for our own benefit. Being good meant never being caught in the street and being very intentional about being seen only inside the house and the yard. In many ways, this stance of being set apart, saved my life. Yet, the friends I might have had from Eastwood saw me behaving as if I was too good for them.

But danger lurked inside the gates too. Our peach house, with its white trim, small front yard adorned by low concrete fencing, was, while beautiful from the outside, hid an ugliness that would rear its head from time to time.

The back of the house was big enough for our family car and flanked by two mango trees, a paw-paw and a lemon tree. In between the trees was concrete flooring that had to be swept and kept clear of the leaves that would fall from the trees. Our neighbours all had similar homes, only distinguished by the care of the small gardens in the front. Families who were better off could be seen maintaining the paint of their homes and maybe even changing colours every so often. The really privileged homes managed to extend their narrow structures and add an additional living room in the place of the front garden or the back yard. But childhoods are shaped by more than the size of a home.

Unfortunately for my siblings and me, the violence was also inside the home. My parents struggled with alcohol addiction.

The heavy drinking would often mean a lack of restraint, translating into excessive beatings with the belt or sticks from the mango trees in the back yard. There were moments when I was thrashed simply because one of my parents – or both of them – had been in a drunken craze. Alcohol addiction was a terrible sickness for parents to struggle with because it locked the entire family into an emotional rollercoaster of guilt, regret and pain.

I don't know when the drinking started, but alcohol was ever-present in our lives. More than just a way of lubricating social interactions like family celebrations, it was everywhere around me. At home, my parents drank almost daily and also sold alcohol as a means of supplementing the family's income. Outside of home, Eastwood was always drunk. From the boys lurking on street corners with bottles strewn at their feet, to the aunties swearing at each other, alcohol was always a feature of this everyday image.

In our home, every beating caused one or more of us to be left with unimaginable bruising that would require us to wear full track suits or long-sleeved jerseys regardless of the weather. It always angered me that these incidents were followed by periods of visible regret and guilt that often looked like my parents were repenting to God, yet without apologising to the child who had been harmed. I never understood how God allowed the violence in the first place and why He kept forgiving my parents after each episode, making available scriptures that could be manipulated to justify violence.

I found coping mechanisms that held me afloat from the beatings. The main thing was not to trigger an incident that could lead to being hit. That meant doing everything as perfectly as I could. The holy grail was doing well at school. My report cards were a source of pride and evidence that the gamble of taking me to a school outside of Eastwood was paying off. Scottsville Primary and later Pietermaritzburg Girls High were both former Model C schools and considered premium, relative to Eastwood Primary and Secondary, though both were closer to home.

Doing well at school had to be accompanied by being the perfect daughter at home. This meant waking up at 4 am with my siblings and helping my mother prepare the food that she'd sell that day. Onions finely diced, chicken pieces cut meticulously, and the balls of dough for *amagwinya* perfectly rounded before being dumped into the pot of boiling oil for deep frying. While some of us prepped and cooked, the others scoured the house from top to bottom. After school I needed to make sure that I was home as early as possible. I was allowed to play sport, but I needed to balance that with the afternoon and evening chores. On arrival home, I'd take off my uniform and socks, wash them and hang them up to dry. Then I'd start the cooking for the evening meal. Today I often chuckle at the realisation that I'm a really good cook because that was what I did every weekday from the moment I was tall enough to stir a pot on a stove until I left home at 18. More than enough practice! But it would be fair to say that I hated this responsibility because I couldn't always control whether it would get me into trouble or not. If the *phuthu* was not fluffy enough, it could lead to being hit. If the curry had too much meat, it was a sign of wastage and could lead to the same fate. I walked this tight rope every evening, praying and hoping that when my parents came home, they'd be sober and find the food to their satisfaction.

My prayer was always the same: 'Lord, you promised me that you will never leave me, and you will never forsake me.' Hebrews 13:5 saved my life many times.

I first met God in a classroom at Eastwood Secondary

school. I was part of a group of young children who had been gathered to participate in Sunday school class led by a neighbour. My parents' own relationship with God had been precarious. We'd done a full 180-degree turn: one day we were a ritual-practising family and the next day we were Christians. I'm not sure what it was that converted my mother to Christianity, but it was certainly a strong force because she not only broke away from all cultural practices that we'd known up till then, she also made it her mission that all of us, starting with my father, would be religious churchgoers who believed completely in the gospel of Jesus Christ.

After every Sunday school class, we were given a verse to recite. I must have received hundreds of Bible verses in those early childhood years but the only one that truly stayed with me, and possibly because it's the one that I've needed the most, is from Hebrews 13 verse 5. The promise was simple: God said that he would never forsake me. This was the only indulgence I allowed myself while letting someone else be in control. I needed to believe that God was ultimately in charge so that I could stay stoic in the moments of hell I'd go through. This verse has carried me through everything that I've needed to survive; it was my lifeline, keeping me positive and resilient, and a guardrail to keep me from losing sight of my belief that things could and would get better. Hebrews 13:5 became my hiding place, allowing me to live the duplicity that my life required. While I was excelling at school and being lauded with different academic, cultural, and sporting accolades, I was hiding scars from my head to my toes. God said He'd never leave me, and I believed it, so

I focused on holding up my side of the deal, getting out and surviving. It took me finding God for myself, and finding my way to therapy, to come to terms with and reconcile some of the experiences I had as a child and to express the love that I have found and continue to sustain for my parents.

When I got to Grade 11 and had the opportunity to choose a university, I didn't even look in my home province. I needed to survive home so that I could escape to my own life.

As my river flowed from high school and childhood to young adulthood and university, it didn't matter to me whether I found myself sleeping under a bridge; I was just not going to be subjected to another day of being perfect, all to avoid a beating, waking up at 4 am, cooking every meal, and being isolated from my friends. University would become my first real escape from the nightmare of an alcohol-fuelled, frenzied family. The time away from home would give me the space to think, speak and act without the fear that my actions would trigger abuse. University would teach me to be my own safe space in a world where I'd come to realise no one else was to be trusted.

FOUR

A *Waskom*, a Mattress and a Loan Shark

We arrived in Pretoria in January 2003.

My mother and I had taken the train from Pietermaritzburg Railway Station: a large building perched at the top of the city with a classic Victorian look-and-feel, ornate finishings hanging like doilies from the corners of the red brick structure.

A central node in the region of KwaZulu-Natal, the station serviced several major cities in the country, transporting almost four million long-distance passengers around the country every year.

Over and beyond its stand-out aesthetic, Pietermaritzburg Railway Station's claim to fame was that in 1893 Mahatma Gandhi, the leader of the nonviolent resistance movement for Indian liberation from the English, had come to the country to act as legal counsel to a merchant. He was thrown off the train because he was seated in the first-class compartment reserved for white passengers only. This confrontation with colonial South Africa sparked in Gandhi the conviction to take up his fight against racism. Although some scholars today argue that Gandhi was inherently racist and advocated Indian rights above all other rights, often at the expense of black African rights, standing on the platform with my mother, a small duffle bag between us, I was inspired to go and fight my own fight, to go further than anyone in my family had.

This moment would come full circle nine years later when I found myself in Mumbai in 2011 as part of my work orientation for the Tata Group. I had some free time in between meetings and decided to visit a local museum, the Mani Bhavan Gandhi *Sangrahalaya*, which was just a few hundred metres down the road from the hotel I was staying. And there, in the middle of Mumbai, was a perfect miniature model of the Pietermaritzburg Railway Station and the story of the origins of Gandhi's fight against racism. Standing as I was in the shadow of Ghandi's inspiration, this was the beginning of my new life as a university student that no one else in my family had travelled. This was the origin of my own fight to get myself out of the poverty I was born into.

I have no recollection of the nine-hour trip from Pietermaritzburg to Pretoria Central Station. I probably regaled my mother with imaginary stories of what university would be like. I suspect we may have dreamed together in between snatches of sleep on our upright, cheap seats, thinking about how the degree I would one day graduate with would be the magic wand that would turn our family's fortunes around. My mother would never have missed an opportunity to reinforce the last lessons and warnings that she and my father had been sharing with me as my departure date crept closer.

'*Ungalahli okukhona ngokungeko.*'

'*Abafana osathane! Bazokuphuca ikusasa lakho.*'

My parents did not send me off with affirmations and affection. Instead, they ensured that I carried a fear of boys, likening them to the devil who comes to steal your dreams away, and a fear of failing my family that would result in unbearable shame for them. This was an effective way of putting up guardrails that would ensure self-control on my part, keep me focused on why I had left home and nothing outside of this. After nine hours, the train delivered us to our final destination, Pretoria Central Station or, more commonly, just Bosman, after the street it was on.

Bosman was a hive of activity as thousands of people were getting on and off trains, and it was abuzz with the hectic sounds of commuters. I heard snippets of languages and accents I had never heard before, all from black Africans who made up the eclectic mix of cultures in Pretoria. I think we stood for a good five minutes, not sure what our next steps needed to be. We eventually followed the crowd away from the platform, into the bright streets of Pretoria, and soon saw the trail of passengers making their way towards the rank where minibus taxis collected passengers from the train and carried them to their next destination.

The taxi rank is the nerve centre of every city in South Africa. Minibus taxis were a response to segregated transportation systems in apartheid South Africa. Black South Africans had restricted access to public transport services, leading to the rise of informal taxi services to meet our transportation needs. Interestingly, the taxi rank became a central connection point for black South Africans. The breaking of a new day was announced by the hooting of taxis looking for early risers who were headed to their jobs, often as early as 4 am. Perfectly synched to the movements between home, work and school, the taxi industry became the pulse of black people's daily experience. This perfect synchronisation sometimes took violent turns as routes became contested as competition in the industry grew. Nonetheless, taxi drivers and taxi owners commanded and received respect, irrespective of the city one was in. They were also trusted custodians of the lost who were seeking directions. We pounced on the first taxi driver we saw to help us plan our next steps.

'*Umntanami uyofunda ePitoli nabelungu. Sicela indawo yokuhlala. Siqale ngakuphi?*'

Only now, in my adult years, when I reflect on this conversation, do I realise how much was said in so few words. My mother managed to convey the significance of this moment for me and for our family, to portray the pride, fear and hope that she and my father felt in this moment, and to successfully transfer to this man we'd just met two minutes earlier the responsibility for finding me a place to stay. He clearly heard her heart and decided to help. He told us of a township called Mamelodi that had student accommodation for women who were from outside of Gauteng. He pointed out the taxi that would take us to Mamelodi and called the owner of the student accommodation who would receive us. My mother took over the call to ascertain for herself that she was not putting me, or both of us, in danger, negotiated the rent downwards and confirmed that I'd be moving in that afternoon. We would have to arrive with cash in hand for the first three months, a foldable mattress, a blanket and a *waskom* in which I could bathe. The taxi driver pointed us a few metres down the road to a vendor selling mattresses and *waskoms* on the pavement. I was all set. The conversation with the taxi driver was a million moons removed from the conversations about residences and apartments that I'd heard some of my friends having, as they swapped stories of their preparations for university. But I could not control what other people had; I could only focus on my own belongings and try to make the most of it.

Mindful that we needed to board a taxi to Mamelodi, and planning so we would not take up extra space requiring fare for an additional seat, we opted for a thin mattress and blanket that could be rolled up and that fitted under my arm and a small green *waskom* that could never hold my whole body in it. In just under an hour, we arrived to a rich mix of cultures and languages, predominantly Sotho and Tswana – not that I could tell the difference then.

Established in the 1950s as a designated township under apartheid, Mamelodi had a rich history of resistance against apartheid policies. It became a hub for political activism, contributing to the broader struggle for freedom in South Africa. But before the football lovers crucify me, Mamelodi was and remains best known for its formidable football club, Mamelodi Sundowns!

We found the house without too much trouble. It was an

unfinished construction site: a double-storeyed maze of bed-rooms that looked like it had been a sprawling mansion for a large family, abandoned mid-construction, to capitalise on the financial opportunity of housing students attending the newly consolidated universities in the province.

The consolidation of higher education institutions in 2002 was part of a broader reform of the higher education system. The aim was to transform universities in the post-apartheid era by improving the quality of output while broadening access for all South Africans. Thirty-six institutions were merged and consolidated into 21 universities to create larger and more comprehensive institutions. More significantly, this was an attempt to transform the historically black, white and Technikon institutions into universities that reflected the diversity of the country, able to redress the historical inequalities that had been rooted in the apartheid system. The mergers were intended to optimise resources and bring quality higher education within reach of people like me. The mergers also meant that some of the existing campuses would become satellites of the newly formed institutions. There was an excitement about these changes in some corners and deep resistance in others that feared consolidation would mean a loss of identity and a drop in quality.

These were the least of my problems, though I had an acceptance letter from the University of Pretoria, and now I needed to get on with the job of turning this opportunity into a life-changing investment for my whole family.

The room I was shown had eight single beds, four on each

side of the room, facing each other. Each of the eight beds had neatly folded blankets, a pillow and under each bed a suitcase of clothes and a personal *waskom*. The eighth bed with its sprightly springs was waiting for my mattress. This was my new home. I was shown to a large but dark bathroom. I quickly understood that the shower was to be the storage place for our *waskoms* and the place we would bathe, but not for actual showering. I was so excited by the prospect of living away from home, making my own decisions, and being part of the University of Pretoria that it didn't matter that, despite the fact that it was shared with siblings, I'd slept in a bigger bed at home. I wasn't perturbed by the fact that I had to bathe in a *waskom*, because although we all shared one bath at home, most of my extended family washed in this manner. This was not new to me. We'd never had a shower at home, and I'd only showered a handful of times at school camps or when visiting white friends.

In the opposite hallway was a shared kitchen. There was no fridge, just a four-plate stove and empty cupboards. It was clear that this was an 'each for herself' set-up. I was prepared. In this mini tour with my mother still present, she whispered warnings to not accept any food offered to me, lest one of my roommates tried to poison me through witchcraft!

I had always been brave. I'd always followed through with whatever was needed even when I was afraid. But in the moment, after our short tour was done and my mother turned to leave, and said '*asihlulwa ilutho thina*', I felt the tears stinging my eyelids. I was alone in a new city, living with people I was yet to meet, and about to start a journey that no one close to me had ever embarked upon. There was an awkward hug. There were no loving words, just a wad of cash, tightly rolled and thrust into my hand, and a reminder that I had come from people who were not easily defeated. No one in my family had ever been to university, so I had no one with whom to navigate this first-in-family experience. My mother, too, was living out her first experience of preparing a child for university.

I was well aware that this was the moment in which I was receiving the reins of control over my own life.

My roommates arrived as the sun was setting and the evening in the township was taking hold. I was too scared to go out, but I could hear the taxis arriving and spilling out weary passengers, returning from work in the city. I heard children trudging home, shuffling feet weighed down by heavy school bags from the fancy schools they attended in the city. I heard the enterprising young men selling onions and tomatoes in micro packages, just enough for one evening meal, marketing directly to the mothers stepping out of the taxis and off the trains, already thinking ahead to the evening meal. My roommates trickled in from the various institutions at which they were studying. I learnt new names: Kutlwano, Tshegofatso, Sarah, and others that have turned to dust in the memory box. From bags emerged ingredients for pap and gravy, maybe an egg to be fried and eaten with slices of bread. Each woman was fending for herself. I didn't have any of that, so that night I slept without eating and settled with the decision that I'd eat on campus the next day.

I woke early the next morning, made my bed, wiped down my body in the *waskom*, and went to find the main campus of the university. I learnt that a few other girls were also enrolled at the main campus and they'd figured out taking the train from Mamelodi station to Hatfield station was a fraction of the cost of a taxi, so I joined them. The wad of cash my mother had given me was five hundred rand. I knew that I could not ask for any more until it was offered.

My first task on campus was to ensure that I was registered for the National Student Financial Aid Scheme (NSFAS). This was the final hurdle I needed to clear to get a foot into the lecture halls.

A few years earlier, in 1996, the government had thrown a funding lifeline to poor students as part of the broader transformation agenda. The promise was simple: prove that you're poor enough to be supported with funding, perform well in your studies, and a portion of your loan will be converted into a grant. I had never been on a university campus before. The buildings were bigger than I'd imagined. There were old buildings that looked like the kind of structures I'd read about in history books. These stood between new, sleek ones that jutted at angles and had large glass doors. Some of the buildings had Afrikaans names engraved or plastered on them, reflecting the history of the institution. I was mesmerised by the sheer size of the library. From the outside it looked to be a few stories high, and I was excited and eager to get in and discover all that it had to offer. But, first, I had to prove that I was smart enough to be there and poor enough to be supported. The NSFAS office was the final line I needed to cross before I could claim my seat in the lecture hall and lose myself in the library.

It had been a painstaking process gathering the documentation the NSFAS officer required. My parents and I had gone to the police station to write several affidavits, swearing under oath that my mother was not formally employed but made a living as a street vendor and that my father was a security guard who earned weekly wages in cash and therefore could not present a pay slip. We had queued for bank statements to get a printout proving there were no material deposits or withdrawals to speak of. I had carefully collected all of these documents together with my acceptance letter and put them in a brown envelope, one that I held tightly as the long, snaking queue inched forward throughout the day. I was among the last to be helped. I hadn't eaten the night before and I'd been too scared to leave my spot in line to get food that day. I'm not sure whether my dry lips betrayed the emptiness of my stomach or if it was the determination on my face, but the officer helping me assured me that my application was strong. All I had to do was present proof of payment of my registration fees. I was floored! I thought that NSFAS would cover the R2 400 registration fee. With a slow, sad shake of his head, I realised that I was not the only one he'd had to break the news to that day. I felt blindsided. How had I missed this? How had I dropped such an important ball? Tears of anger flowed as I stepped out of the air-conditioned building and back into the dry and now-dimmed heat of

the sun. I was mad at myself because I was one of the students that really needed this lifeline to study. It was an
extraordinary amount of money for my family, and I knew
that my parents didn't have it. I felt like all my dreams were
flatlining.

I called my mother, explaining the feedback. I think I was
expecting resignation from her and a mirroring of the defeat
I was feeling in my spirit. My mother only repeated the words
she'd left me with a few days ago, *'asihlulwa ilutho thina.'*

I stayed in Mamelodi for the next three days as my parents hustled for the registration fee. My parents tried their
siblings. One of my aunts was a nurse, her husband a police-
man, and one of my uncles worked in a cotton factory. All
three had pay slips, but none was willing to put it up as collateral for a bank loan for my required registration fee. A girl
at university was too risky an investment. Ma was told 'if
only she was a boy, it would be easier' and 'what's the use
of all this studying if she's going to get married and build
someone else's family?'

My mother would later tell me that a visit to a loan shark,
a withdrawal from the *stokvel* and subtle blackmail of one of
her customers, had raised the required funds. Loan sharks
have always thrived in black communities in South Africa.
Historically starved from access to formal banking services
because of credit histories that didn't fit the mould of formal banking institutions' credit-lending models, loan sharks
stepped in to meet the need for immediate access to funds.
The exorbitant interest rates were an accepted trade-off against
the need for cash, creating temporary safety nets that often

locked lenders into a vicious cycle of dependency. A third of my registration fee came from a local loan shark.

Stokvels – a club for people who contribute fixed sums on a regular basis into a fund that acts as a rotating lending union or savings plan – were another form of buffer against shocks for poor families in South Africa. For as long as I can remember, my mother was always a member of a *stokvel*. This was one of the saving mechanisms that we relied on, but, more importantly, in crisis, my mother could also borrow against her social standing in the *stokvel*. The only criterion was that members needed to trust that any money borrowed would be paid back as promised. The second third of the fee came from the *stokvel*. Years later at business school, I'd sit in a lecture on microfinance as part of my studies in development finance and be told that this type of social lending originated in Bangladesh in the 70s. I wondered if Muhammad Yunus, who went on to found the Grameen Bank on this model, and received a Nobel Peace Prize for this invention in 2006, knew that social lending was as old as the wrinkles on my *khokho's* skin.

My mother was highly entrepreneurial. In addition to the sales of food she made as a street vendor, our home fridge was stocked with 750 ml bottles of Black Label and Castle Lager beer for sale, *depending on who was asking*. The sale of alcohol in this form was illegal, but in our street alone my mother had two competitors in the trade. If there ever was a falling out among the three traders, you would see a police van pull up to raid the home being targeted. So we were taught to sell beer only to people we knew. *uMalume*

Zondi was one of her regulars. He ran a monthly tab that his wife didn't know about and which he would settle at the end of each month. To keep the discretion and the promise of payment, my mother held his ID book among at least a dozen others in one of her bedside drawers. I didn't know how she convinced him to put up his pay slip to raise the last third, but I wouldn't put a little blackmail past her.

I rejoined the NSFAS line on the fourth day, this time with every requirement in hand – and a full tummy. I finally got my approval. The doors to the rest of my life swung open. My parents had done everything they could, now it was all up to me. My river had carried me faithfully and steadily from uncertain beginnings as I stood waiting for the university gates to open, but from here the river was flowing freely into my new life. The reins of control were now fully in my hands and I held on tightly. The rest of my life could begin.

FIVE

The War within

Wthen I left home, I thought the war was over. I had not bargained that the war within me would continue to rage.

I soon realised that living in Mamelodi while attending lectures in Hatfield was not sustainable: it was far, I got to school dusty from walking to the train station and back, and the train schedule meant that I couldn't stay as long as I needed in the library. In addition, I'd seen one too many petty crimes while in transit, chains snatched off necks, cell phones grabbed from the user in mid-sentence, and a knife fight that had all of us scurrying on moving carriages. I needed to find alternative accommodation.

While I envied other students who stayed at the university residences – each building with an Afrikaans name, bright uniforms that singled them out from the rest of us, holding cards they could swipe for food multiple times a day, and needing only to walk between their rooms and their lectures – I knew I couldn't afford more debt by applying to NSFAS to fund my accommodation. I'd seen my family struggle with finances all my life and getting into debt was not an option I was willing to consider. I never wanted money to control what I could or couldn't do because I'd seen that play out far too many times at home. I started asking around for opportunities to share apartments with other students. The surrounding areas close to campus like Hatfield and Arcadia were far too expensive and completely out of reach even if I was to share with four other students. The search was very quickly narrowed down to Sunnyside.

I'd heard Sunnyside being described as the place of the devil. I soon learnt that the description was accurate. Apart from students from all over the continent, Sunnyside was a dense population of drug dealers, prostitutes, beggars and many types of unsavoury characters. I had to be economical with my description of this place when I told my parents I'd be moving from Mamelodi and into a bachelor flat with two other girls. I mediated the narrative by highlighting that the distance from campus was shorter and cheaper, and would allow me to spend more time in the library. What closed the deal was that I also committed to paying my own rent. Sold! I rolled up my mattress for the last time in Mamelodi, left my *vaskom* in the dark bathroom and took a taxi to central Pretoria and then another to Sunnyside.

While I was making plans to move to Sunnyside, I also made plans to get a job in order to hold up my end of the bargain of paying my own rent. I walked into a restaurant called La Pat on a Thursday afternoon after lectures and approached the man who looked like the owner. Joe De Freites and his father were Portuguese nationals who'd just opened the restaurant in Hatfield. Their business model was perfect for me: hire students, let them earn through their tips, give them the flexibility they needed to keep studying, and – more importantly, as far as my rent was concerned – pay them 2% of all the sales they'd made during the month.

I'd never waited on tables before, but Joe didn't seem concerned. He was comfortable that I could speak English well and that I seemed to have the right attitude. La Pat soon became a big part of my survival strategy. It allowed me to cut the strings of financial dependence on my family and it bought me time and space to heal. I now had a legitimate excuse not to go home during the holidays: I was working. The real reason, of course, was that I was afraid that I'd walk back into the trauma of beatings. After months of living alone, I was finally discovering myself beyond the restrictions imposed by my parents and I was not prepared to relinquish that feeling. In truth, I didn't realise then that I was just transferring the control my parents had held over my life to a new form, one that I was now imposing upon myself.

Waiting tables taught me some of my most important business lessons. I learnt what it really meant to put customers at the centre of the experience being delivered. On days that I didn't get this right I'd make fewer tips and generate fewer sales. I learnt the importance of being the energy you want others to embody. If I was bubbly and engaging, my customers would be open and engaging too. I signed up for most weekend shifts at La Pat, leaving campus on Friday afternoons to wait on students who had the means to frequent restaurants after a tough week of lectures and assignments. On Saturdays I put in a double shift to catch the early morning families visiting their children in the surrounding residences, and I stayed until the late-night drinking crowd arrived, out for a good time on a Saturday night. Sunday morning was a huge money-maker. The after-church crowd, generous from their sermons, would tip healthily. In this way, I made enough money to cover my rent, buy food and photocopy the textbooks that other students could afford to purchase. On months when I did exceptionally well, I sent money to my parents to help out and to reinforce why I wasn't coming home as much. I quickly learnt that money kept the questions about my absence at bay, so I sent as much as I could. My younger sisters were now transitioning to university too, so I knew that even a thousand rand would make a difference. I exercised tight discipline over my time. Weekends were for making money, weekdays were for school. The plan was to keep the schedule tight, to keep my head down and to put in the work where it was required.

When campus closed for the holiday season over Easter or Christmas, I'd stay behind. Sunnyside would become eerily quiet and most students left for home. I relished this silence and quiet time alone. The restaurant wasn't busy during these periods either and that meant I had a lot of time to study and get ahead and to simply be alone. I'd sleep in, read and just be. I was also unlearning some of the unhealthy coping mechanisms I'd developed at home.

While on the surface it looked like my river was flowing smoothly, there were underlying currents. I had a distorted image of my weight. I had always seen myself as fat and had, in fact, suffered from bulimia throughout my high school years. Finding solace in food, I would eat more than what my body required. This dulled the pain of the beatings at home.

While I was actively struggling with my illness in high school, the seeds had been planted as early as primary school. I had transitioned into a white school environment while my body was also transitioning into puberty. My thick, hairy legs and generous arms didn't fit the description of beauty in that new environment. While my family assured me that I was beautiful, all I wanted was skinny, hairless, straight legs like all the other girls around me. I had also read a book in primary school, *The Best Little Girl in the World*, by Steven Levenkron. It was meant to be a warning about the negative effects of bulimia and how, if left unmanaged, it might lead to the more serious condition of anorexia nervosa. Except I didn't read the book as intended by the author. I dug into it as if it were a how-to guide on managing my weight. I saw myself in the main character's struggle and so I mimicked her. I learnt to use my fingers after binge eating to regurgitate the contents of my stomach. I knew that I needed to run the bathroom taps to mask the sound of my meal being brought up and that I could chew my food and then spit it out without swallowing to trick my brain into thinking I was eating. I learnt that laxatives kept my stomach flat and skipping meals got me closer to my goal weight faster. I tried to restrict my eating and jumped on every diet I heard of. All this yo-yo dieting led to overall weight gain that compromised my health, but was an even greater emotional weight on my heart.

Placing my body under such restraint seemed to be the one thing I could fully own while I was still at home. Weight gain and loss were proxies for being in, and out, of control. When I gained weight, I was in freefall and most likely treading in emotional quicksand. When I lost a few kilograms, it was because I'd restricted my eating, binged and over-exercised, and felt most in control. For years after I left home, I was stuck on this rollercoaster and had no way of coming off it. The time alone in Pretoria was the gear I needed to slow down the rollercoaster ride, but I had not yet found the switch to turn it off altogether. I knew I was sick; I had done enough reading to know that what I was doing was not normal. But my distorted self-image kept a tight hold over my life. I felt too embarrassed to talk to anyone about this, especially because I thought it ridiculous that a poor black person had time to be struggling with body issues. The people I knew had real sicknesses like HIV Aids or tuberculosis. I had always feared that if I were found out, my parents would beat the sickness out of me.

In the shared apartment in Sunnyside, I started cooking for myself, took the decision to confront my body distortion issues and to try and to get better. I thought recovering meant losing the weight once and for all, yet I had no idea that although the sickness manifested in my body, it was actually festering in my mind too. I joined a gym and started exercising and discovered a love for running. I also learnt that smoking weed could help me finally shed the weight, provided I took a walk before the onset of the munchies! I'd never seen a chubby person who smoked weed regularly, so I tried it.

These interventions were not all healthy, but they put me back in the driving seat to some extent and helped me heal in ways I didn't know that I needed. I lost 16 kg in one year and vowed to stay vigilant, eating healthier and exercising, in an effort never to gain it back. Of course, this also meant that if I jumped on the scale and saw the numbers ticking up, I'd go into an emotional free fall and sign up to a new diet. I had learnt how to survive my external environment, from my community to my parents, and now I was only beginning to learn how to survive myself. The war with control was no longer being waged outside of me with other people, it was raging *inside and against me.*

Exam season was tough. While many people who went to Tuks might associate the vivid images of Jacaranda trees lining the streets in Pretoria with exam season, for me, exam season was always marked by hunger. I couldn't take on as many shifts at the restaurant as I needed because I had to allocate most of my time to studying. I knew that the only way to survive was to focus on what mattered most: studying and working just enough to pay the rent and buy whatever food I could afford after the bills were settled. My go-to meal on most of these days was bread and sugar. One of the girls I shared the flat with had brought a sandwich-maker with her, intended for slices of bread lined with cheese and other yummy ingredients. We figured out that by sprinkling sugar on the bread and then placing it in the sandwich maker, the sugar melted, creating a syrupy-like substance and a 'jam sandwich'.

I would often have to walk from campus, 4 km each way, because I couldn't afford the bus ticket in those times. It was on one of those walks, trudging down Church Street, with my backpack on, that my life took a destiny-defining turn.

It had been a tough month. The demands of my university studies had heightened, so I had not had the opportunity to fit in many working weekends. For those who know Pretoria well, you will know that Church Street runs almost the breadth of Pretoria, from Hatfield all the way through to town. As I approached the back of the Sheraton Hotel – the Union Buildings to my right and the hotel on my left – the next steps that I took that day completely changed my life.

I remember seeing the advert: it stood out because it had a large emblem of the government coat of arms, and was stuck on the wall at the back of the hotel. I can't tell you what it was that made me pay attention to the posters that day. Perhaps my eye was caught by the official-looking document; I realised that it was an advert calling for applications for the presidency's internship programme.

The advert, however, was smack bang in the middle of two blue and white penis enlargement posters. These sorts of poster were familiar to South Africans and recognisable a mile away for the colours used, the same-sized font, the offer of all sorts of services: from how to bring back lost lovers to magic potions to ensure that your lover lost interest in all others! It just didn't make sense to me how the highest seat of government, an iconic landmark that represents the political life of South Africa in all its beauty, sprawling across the breadth of the gorgeous gardens decorating this national heritage site, would advertise on the back of a hotel. Had someone from the human resources department really made their way down the buildings' elegant exterior steps, past the statues of Nelson Mandela and Louis Botha, navigated the many indigenous trees scattered throughout the grounds, walked through the main gates, crossed Church Street and, finally, with glue stick and poster in hand, still chosen the space between two penis enlargement announcements? I just couldn't believe it. I still don't.

I took off my backpack, felt around for a notepad and a pen, and decided that even if it was the most unlikely and ridiculous thing to do that day, no harm could come from it. I went to the university's computer centre the next morning and applied for my place on the internship programme before going to my first lecture. I heard nothing for six months. I'd all but forgotten about the application when, in the middle of my honours year, I got a call from a lady saying that she was part of the HR department at the presidency and that she was inviting me to an interview. I honestly thought it was a prank call at first, but soon realised that it was legitimate. She set the interview for the following day!

I had dreadlocks in my hair – the best low-maintenance hairstyle for any student on a very tight budget – and from everything I knew about interviews, I'd have to find a way to tame them to look presentable in less than 24 hours. With my thin locks in a tight bun, I needed to find an outfit fit for the presidency. With my budget, it meant going to Mr Price and picking out a pair of low, black kitten heels, a pair of grey pants and a white shirt. I'd later graduate in this exact same outfit a year later when I completed my honours degree.

The next morning, I made my way up to the offices of the president. The closer I got, the more imposing the buildings became. I hadn't known that the Union Buildings actually sat on the highest point in Pretoria, and I was not anticipating the arduous, steep climb to the top. Designed in the English monument style, the 285 m-long semi-circular offices had two wings on each of the east and west wing sides. These wings represented the union of a formerly divided people. The statue of President Nelson Mandela stood on the exact spot where he gave his inaugural address on 10 May in 1994.

The climb got even steeper as I passed the amphitheatre towards the glass doors. To say that I had underestimated the distance I needed to walk would be a gross underestimation! I arrived soaked with sweat; I could literally feel it running down my back as my white shirt stuck to my body. I eventually made it to the glass doors, where I was subjected to an extensive security check, and then beyond the point up until which tourists are allowed and into the sanctuary of the red-brick building.

It was vast and everything seemed to loom over me. There was an incredible amount of light and air on the inside of the Union Buildings, provided by the inner courtyards that connected the different wings of the building. The interior design paid homage to the Cape Dutch architectural style, with carved teak fanlights, heavy doors and dark ceiling beams. The arches of the corridors, the thickness of the curtains and even the polite clinking of the mobile tea tray as one of the workers passed me with tea and treats on the most delicate and beautiful china I'd ever seen, combined to embed a sense of gravitas in me.

I was escorted to a meeting room where I'd wait to be called, joining at least a dozen other interviewees. As my sweat settled and turned my skin cold, I was nervous and on edge as I took in how everyone was much older than me. I was called in and faced the first interview panel I'd ever encountered, with at least ten officials representing different functions in the presidency.

I did my best. The years of public speaking, debating, Toastmasters and wooing clients on the restaurant floor kicked in. I paced myself as eloquently and convincingly as I could. I got the call a few days later: I'd been hired as one of 15 young people to join the presidency and, more importantly, I was handpicked for the Private Office of the Deputy President.

SIX

Ma'am

When the writers of African proverbs spoke about how it took a village to raise a child, they must also have meant that a child was raised by multiple parents, each showing up at different stages of their life. My parents had gone as far as their own imaginations could stretch. They had raised me beyond what they had achieved for themselves, but they could not raise me *beyond what they could comprehend* for themselves. My next mother would stretch me past whatever point might once have seemed unimaginable for someone like me.

I did not expect to be assigned to the Private Office of the Deputy President, Phumzile Mlambo-Ngcuka, nor did I anticipate that the deputy president herself would work with me and take an interest in me. I certainly had no expectation that she'd become a mentor. Yet she was all this and more.

When I arrived in the Private Office of the Deputy President, I was warmly welcomed by a large contingent of leaders, all of them reporting to the deputy president. I didn't know that I'd be working with all of them. I should have read the enthusiasm as a sign that I'd be doing a lot of running around and learning from everyone! I was also going to be spending a considerable amount of time with the deputy president herself. We called her DP or Ma'am, interchangeably. It was just the right balance of intimacy and formality.

There have been countless moments where Ma'am reminded me that I was destined to be more than what I or others saw in me in the moment. In big and small ways, she stood in the gap and believed in me, as well as *for me*, when my life's experiences were not able to stretch me past what I'd seen and experienced.

As the intern in the office, I was the runaround for everyone. But the gift of that running around was that I got close to the portfolios of each of the leaders in the Private Office. Under Ambassador Zolile Magugu I became familiar with the work of the DP in international relations. I had studied this and was thrilled to see international relations at play beyond the textbooks that I had read during my studies. Suddenly, I had a front-row seat to observe how countries and global institutions engaged, how power was traded and how bilateral negotiations took place. When I was allowed in the room during some meetings, I always had to produce a written report for Ma'am about what I'd learnt. I learnt a lot about protocol, too, and particularly the spoken and unspoken rules that determined the pecking order of power in a given setting. As the youngest and most junior person in all of the rooms I was invited into, I would happily take up my seat closest to the door, the kitchen or the bathroom – what mattered was that I was in the room.

I met other deputy presidents, presidents, ambassadors and diplomats, heads of global organisations, leaders in civil society and captains of industry. I saw the government machinery set in motion to ensure that Ma'am was prepared and armed with the relevant information to engage other heads and deputy heads of state. I saw the importance of looking the part, the careful selection of her attire for each occasion. I also witnessed her insistence on wearing her natural hair, cut short or in neat cornrows, on any and every stage. Without ever having to have the conversation, the lessons about owning and embracing being African in global spaces landed quickly. Our lessons extended beyond the workplace and she'd land teachings I didn't even know I needed.

'*Isikhwama sentombazane asikhamisi!*'

I learnt poise, posture, and even how to carry my handbag like a proper lady.

The late Ayanda Nkuhlu was one of Ma'am's advisors. He was the ultimate diplomat and the bridge between our political principal and the team. He called everyone *Mtshana*! He awakened in me the idea of humility as a leadership style. This was my first time seeing black excellence in abundance in the workplace. The DP's diary-meeting was a sacred space that I was allowed to sit in and observe – just listen, without being permitted any contribution. I watched real-time trade-offs being made in a high-profile political office about where she could be, when and where she could not, and why this was the case. I observed how those decisions were made and, more importantly, how they were communicated to the various stakeholders, especially to those entities whose requests for her presence had been declined. Ayanda would check every piece of correspondence to a declined invitation and thereby taught all of us the importance of letting people down with kindness and respect.

From Bongi Kunene, who joined the team as chief of staff and would later go on to become the executive director at the World Bank Group in Washington, I learnt accountability. A promise made is a promise to be kept, she reminded us. She read all of my reports and encouraged me to write more proactively so that I could become a contributing member to the team who prepared background notes for the DP. When now-minister Nkhensani Kubayi joined the Private Office as special projects director, she must have been the youngest woman, other than me, on the team. She brought me close when planning the DP's *imbizo* visits to different communities, from which I learnt the importance of centring people in policy formulation. It was a masterclass in accountability. In every community we visited the DP had to account to mamas, *gogos*, chiefs and young people, gathered to hear what the government was doing to resolve the challenges with which they were confronted. No issue was too small to be addressed. There was no better place to observe the power of allowing people to be heard and seen.

I watched how Raisibe Morathi and Nonhlanhla Mjoli-Mncube, the economic advisors to the DP, wrestled with the

Accelerated and Shared Growth Initiative for South Africa (ASGISA), and what it really took to translate economic policy aspirations into real economic growth. Growth rates were between 4% and 5% in the early 2000s, urban skylines were dotted with cranes, reflecting expanding infrastructure investments, and small and medium-sized enterprises were centred as government looked to ease the knots of red tape that made doing business a challenge for entrepreneurs. It's not lost on me that my first encounter with power and leaders who held considerable influence over the shaping of the South African economy were black and mostly women.

I also got very close to Ma'am's personal assistants, Elizabeth Taylor and Khosi Shange. They became the big sisters I never had and took care of me over and beyond what was required. My biggest lesson from them was to pay meticulous attention to detail. They checked and rechecked schedules, flight paths, presidential protection unit assignments, coordination with the household staff – all with crisp communication to lock in clarity and alignment. Our office mantra was 'it's not done until it's done'. This meant that we made zero assumptions. If an email had been sent, it didn't mean that the message had been received or understood. Only a clear confirmation from the receiver provided comfort that the job was indeed finally done. This is one of the first things I share with new hires in my office today, and I'm relentless about it.

Sis Doreen Kosi's office became my base when I arrived. She'd organised a small desk in her office for me to work from. She remains solely responsible for my unhealthy relationship with coffee! Beyond caffeine, she taught me the

importance of protocol, how it levels the expectations of behaviour in political settings and, done correctly, can go a
long way in facilitating diplomatic relations, decorum and
respect.

God seemed to handpick leaders with an exceptional work
ethic for me over the years. Ma'am set the tone for me and
the team. She led by example. I cannot ever recall her leaving
us in the office to go and rest if there was still work to be
done. On the days when she was not in the office or in one
of her many engagements, she was receiving guests at the
official residence. We always knew it would be a long night
when she kicked off her shoes and walked around her office
barefoot. We knew to kick off our high heels, too, and put
our shoulders to the wheel. At times we'd need to be ready
to travel as early as 2 am depending on where she needed to
be. These were the best times of my life! I was privileged to
have seen it and experienced it at such a young age: my early
twenties. It set the foundation for my own expectations for
myself and for those I work with today.

Like all government departments, as an intern, I was still
receiving a R2 500 stipend. I spent R800 on rental and the rest
on food and clothing. This was a massive cut to my finances
compared to what I'd become accustomed to at the restaurant. But it was also a no-brainer. I didn't think twice about
giving up an average income of R6 000 a month, made from
a combination of my tips and 2% of my monthly sales at the
restaurant, in exchange for the stipend of R2 500.

I'd found another intern who was keen on having a room-mate as this would reduce her rent. Gcino Mlaba let me have her lounge for R800. We put up a flimsy curtain to separate the sitting room from the open-plan kitchen. I was all set. I lived out of my suitcase. I travelled and saw the world with Ma'am and the team and only came back to the apartment for a change of clothes. From South Korea, Ireland, Portugal and India to France, and many places in between, I could not have asked for a better job.

Whenever Ma'am invited me to accompany her on different missions, she'd always make a point of jokingly introducing me with the phrase: 'I am Nozi's bring a girl child to work project,' which, of course, elicited much laughter wherever we went. She still does it today! Yes, it may appear to be just a silly joke, but she didn't have to take me on her travels, she didn't have to introduce me at all, and she certainly didn't have to welcome me in a manner that would warm people to me. It felt to me that the way she treated me privately and publicly signalled to others how I was to be treated. It was a big lesson in how a leader's words and actions were the cue for the way their staff were to be treated by others. Ma'am was destiny-defining in my life. She built on the foundations of self-belief that my mother instilled, broadened my view of myself in the world and widened the world itself to me.

A year into my internship, I was set to graduate from my honours course among the top students in my class. Given the fulltime nature of my work, I'd applied for a six-month extension so I might have a better chance of maintaining good grades as I worked and travelled. It helped that the lectures were in the evening, so I could somewhat balance work and studies. My graduation date had been set and I booked bus tickets for my parents to attend. They arrived off the Greyhound at Bosman station.

Four-and-a-half years earlier, my mother and I had arrived at the very same station to start the journey, and now it was complete. The bet had paid off. I was a graduate and an honours one at that! More importantly, I was working for the deputy president. It was a great story for my parents to tell. Knowing my salary, the team in the Private Office surprised me with a fully paid two-night stay for my parents at the Sheraton Hotel – the very same building that had displayed the poster advertising the internship!

Knowing that we'd be taking lots of pictures and that they'd be staying at a 5-star hotel, my parents went all out. A tan suit for my father against a black shirt and a gold tie; a black knee-length dress for my mother with a black-and-white wrap-around belt to accentuate her figure.

The graduation ceremony was long, but I could feel and hear my parents' pride. Never people to be outdone, I could hear my mother's ululation and my father's accompaniment of the Mbanjwa clan names ring out into the AULA on the university campus:

'*Sokhela!*'
'*Nony'emnyama!*'
'*Eyabizwa ngekhwela yasabela yathi tshiyo!*'
'*Gqabela kavezi!*'

'*Wena ozalisa abafazi baliwe amadoda abo!*'
'*Mzukuzeli ulwandle aluwelwa zinkonjane ezindizela phezulu!*'
'*Sisho wena nkanyezi yezulu!*'
'*Mzekwa!*'
'*Magujwa!*'
'*Dindela!*'
'*Mbanjwa!*'

I received my scroll, got a tap on the head, and walked giddily off stage, waltzing on their pride.

The very next Monday I was called into Ma'am's office. I was still feeling quite chuffed with myself and riding the cloud of the graduation evening as I pushed open the heavy, dark oak doors, crossed the Persian carpet in the large office and took a seat in the chair facing her. Her desk was littered with different briefing folders, indicative of a busy day and intense preparations. She set it all aside and asked about my graduation ceremony and how my parents had experienced it.

'So *Ntombi*, what's next?' I had no idea what she was talking about. Next where?

'I'm sorry Ma'am, what do you mean?'

'When are you doing your master's?'

The blank look on my face must have betrayed me. I was confused. She went on to explain that nobody in her office worked without a plan for how they were achieving their academic goals. Everyone was either registered for something or had just graduated. It didn't matter if it was a six-month certificate or a doctorate, everyone was furthering their education in one way or another. I remembered that she was a teacher in her early professional years and I knew that there was no getting out of this. I wasn't able to answer her question, so she sent me away with homework. In one week, she needed to know what I intended to study, and where. Her parting shot opened the world for me.

'I don't want to see the University of Pretoria on that list! You've done enough there. You're ready to study abroad.'

I returned a week later with a plan to work towards becoming a diplomat. The University of London's School of Oriental and African Studies (SOAS) was at the top of my list. My research revealed that a number of South Africans who had been pivotal in midwifing the country's democracy had gone to SOAS and others were prominent players in business, such as the governor of the South African Reserve Bank (SARB), Lesetja Kganyago, and the former CEO of Absa and then Barclays Africa, Maria Ramos. I was sold. My application went in a few months later. Which is how I came to study at SOAS in London. This was just one of the many moments when Ma'am stood in the gap of belief for me, having faith in me when I could not see beyond where I was standing in that moment. After all, I could imagine a few people asking who the hell I thought I was to even think I could be counted among the alumni of one the most prestigious international relations schools in the world. But there was a woman who knew exactly who I could be, and she made sure that I met that version of myself.

SEVEN

Return on Luck

The one-year, full-time programme at SOAS included a research dissertation that made up 50% of the requirements for a pass. I kept my research area in familiar territory: I wanted to find out how South Africa's economic strength relative to that of neighbour, Zimbabwe, translated into political influence on Zimbabwe's foreign policy. My qualitative research was mined from a bunch of organisations focused on the foreign affairs of countries in the Southern African Development Community (SADC). I was particularly interested in how President Thabo Mbeki and the South African government had been able to influence Zimbabwe's President Robert Mugabe. My interest was sparked by the ongoing media commentary that suggested a tension between an economically strong South Africa and the politically stronger Zimbabwe. I was also intrigued by the politics of seniority on the continent: President Mugabe was considered an elder, one of the early and leading political figures in the fight for liberation on the continent; President Mbeki, on the other hand, an economist trained at Sussex University, was considered intellectually sharp and the face of the new generation of African leaders picking up the baton from the elders.

I soon found my match at SOAS. Michelle Moon-Lim, a Korean-American, would become the twin sister I didn't know I needed.

'South Africa? Which country in South Africa?'

I heard her throaty chuckle escape. She'd overheard me in the lecture hall for the third time trying to explain that South Africa was a country and not a region in Africa. Just looking at her, I suspected that she'd had her fair share of explaining why she looked Chinese and sounded American. I could feel her feeling for me.

'Nelson Mandela?' I offered the enquirer. The mention of the great statesman usually did the trick, but not this time.

'Yes, but which country?' I thanked the heavens that the course coordinator entered the room at that moment and called for our attention.

How on earth was I in an international relations programme with people who didn't know that South Africa was a country? Michelle scooted over and sat next to me.

'Hi,' she whispered out the corner of her mouth and then in a full-blown American accent, 'I'm Mitch. Bloody Americans and their limited geography!'

We were inseparable from day one. As luck would have it, we were assigned to the same student residence too. With our textbooks in hand, and an outline of the semester's modules, we made for the bus stop that would take us to our apartment.

I'd landed at Heathrow a week earlier and spent that first week with a family that Ma'am had asked to extend their home to me and help me acclimatise before the programme started, while Mitch had spent her first week exploring London after a 20-hour flight from Idaho. We were both 'it' in our families: first-born daughters expected to do well and improve the prospects of their families. Her father had emigrated from South Korea and started a business in Idaho. There he met her mother, an American, and they'd had Michelle, just three months after I was born in Pietermaritzburg.

Like me, Mitch came from a family that was no stranger to hard work. While my mother sold food, fruit, cigarettes, and even alcohol from the side of the road, her mother cleaned people's houses to make ends meet. We were both on scholarships. We'd walked into SOAS with nothing but were determined to leave with something. I would learn so much from Mitch. That first evening after we helped each other move into our tiny rooms in an apartment we shared with three other students, we headed out to find groceries together. We shared the apartment with a girl from Ukraine, a boy from Greece, and another boy from London. In that eclectic mix of cultures, our friendship took root and strengthened. The Tesco supermarket was a few metres away from our residence and became the place where we bought our food for the next couple of months. We bonded over the frustration of the exchange rate and the pain of the cost of food in London, and helped each other figure out the underground and the red bus system which enabled us to get around. We made a pact that we'd live as paupers so we could save our stipends and then convert what was left into rands for me, and dollars for Mitch, when we each got back home.

I taught her how to cook chicken curry and she taught me how to make kimchi, and familiarised my tongue with salted seaweed. Our mates in the apartment came from affluent families, allowing them to visit restaurants a few times each week and to take the underground to class. We allowed ourselves only one indulgence: a night out on the last weekend of every month. We'd cook and eat at the apartment first, having only enough money to spend on drinks.

We both loved to dance. I introduced her to kwaito, deep house and later Durban-inspired *gqom*; she taught me all her American R&B dance moves and introduced me to Korean music and drama, long before K-pop and K-drama became a thing. On our nights out we danced until the wee hours and were literally the last ones to leave the dance floor. Sangria, a budget-friendly mix of red wine, fruit and a splash of brandy was our go-to drink, and a jug or two would sort us out for the night. We'd teeter back to the apartment, sharing a piping hot kebab from the street vendors who knew exactly what a London night out needed at 2 in the morning!

Mitch was the first gay person I'd been close to. Growing up, I'd known a few gay people from a distance. The conversation about homosexuality had never featured at home, so

all that I knew I'd learnt from school and from friends. Sometimes Mitch and I would visit lesbian bars together so she
could be in a space that felt safe for her too. We'd have a blast.
She was and remains a beautiful example of living with multiple identities. When I pointed out to her that I was the only
black person in our programme on that first day, she was quick
to land a lesson on diversity:

'Nozi, I'm the only Korean-American here. Sana is the only
person from Ukraine here. I think Andreas is the only Greek
person. We are all carrying some form of identity from wherever we come. You get to choose what being the only black
African woman in the programme is going to mean. It doesn't
have to be the story of apartheid.'

She had a way of challenging the stereotypes I attributed
to myself and to others. It doesn't surprise me one bit that
she went on to become a consultant to help some of the biggest UK-based companies build and implement their diversity, equity, and inclusion policies.

While Mitch and I focused on getting through the programme
as cheaply as we could, I kept an eye on the politics at home.
I had been following a worrisome political development
brewing in South Africa.

Away from the presidency, in between lectures, I caught
up on news of a mounting movement within the African
National Congress to recall President Mbeki. I tried to do the
calculations. If President Mbeki were recalled, would that
mean that the deputy president would be recalled too? If
she were recalled, what would happen to the staff in the DP's

Private Office? What would happen to me? Would I still have a job when I got back from London? Nobody had answers for me. The ANC conference in Polokwane loomed on the horizon in 2009. That would deliver all the answers to this bag-full of questions, and I made the decision to be as close to the outcome as possible. I needed to be in touch with the developments so that I could make decisions with information that was not just gleaned from online media reports. London was too far away.

It was out of genuine interest in the political dynamics of the region as well as a fear of losing my job that I focused my research sample on foreign affairs-facing organisations in South Africa. This allowed me to come home and complete the last few months of research and writing in Pretoria. As I was completing my dissertation, I stayed in close contact with colleagues in the office and got regular updates on the various scenarios that might play out.

* * *

One of the very few people in South African politics to have served under three administrations: the presidencies of Mandela, Mbeki and Zuma, during the period 1995 to 2009, was the Reverend Frank Chikane. His book, *Eight Days in September: The recall of Thabo Mbeki*, is a riveting account of the eight-day period that led to President Mbeki's recall. When the Mandela administration took to the Union Buildings in 1994, Chikane was appointed as the Director-General in the

Office of the Deputy President, Thabo Mbeki. When President Mbeki took the reins of the presidency in 1997, Chikane moved with him and became Director-General in the Office of the President.

As I sat in my apartment in Pretoria in 2008, there was no way of knowing how much the reverend was managing the backend as the country teetered on the edge of yet another transition. In his book, and on a number of platforms on which he's been interviewed, he detailed the decision of the Pietermaritzburg High Court on 12 September 2008 to set aside the corruption charges against the then deputy president, Jacob Zuma, as the beginning of the end for Mbeki, and the ascent of Zuma to the presidency. Mounting support for Jacob Zuma could not be denied. The ANC's National Conference in Polokwane the previous December had already elected Zuma as the president of the party, while President Mbeki retained his position as president of the country. The two-headed leadership posture could not hold for long, though. Once the courts had cleared Zuma of corruption charges, as far as some ANC members were concerned, the onus was on President Mbeki to leave the position of state president.

Chikane wrote that in the early hours of 20 September 2008 President Mbeki was informed of the decision of the ANC to remove him. He wrote about the stoic way in which President Mbeki received the news, and that without any show of emotion he accepted the decision and enquired only about the most constitutionally correct way to effect his resignation. The rest of us found out about the president's intention to resign on national television the next day.

In a broadcast message just shy of 15 minutes, President Mbeki made clear his intention to submit to parliament his letter of resignation and to enable a peaceful transition for the incoming administration. Chikane let us in on the many celebrations that had been planned to mark the end of the second term of President Mbeki's presidency, which then had to be cancelled. His term was meant to have ended in seven months, but the recall clearly could not wait.

Chikane's book captured the chronological events of that week, but also the anxiety and fear that must have flowed through the corridors of the Union Building's east and west wings as everyone tried to find their footing in the quicksand of the moment. The news cycle was gathering at a whip-lashing pace, with every outlet focusing on the unexpected resignation.

I did not foresee the next chess play coming. For 48 hours I had imagined the different scenarios playing out at the Union Buildings. Would Ma'am become president and make history as the first woman president of South Africa? Would the staff in the office of the deputy president become the staff of the president? Would I be working for the president now? My confirmation bias towards a 'woman-making-history' narrative blindsided me completely to the events that were to follow. On 23 September 2008, the country was rocked by the news that Ma'am had resigned along with ten other ministers and deputy ministers: Minister in the Presidency Essop Pahad, Minister of Defence Mosiuoa Lekota, Minister of Intelligence Ronnie Kasrils and the Deputy Minister of Finance, Jabu Moleketi, among others, submitted their resignations to the president. In the mayhem of all these political developments, I hurried to finish my research and submit my dissertation. I was too scared to call or text Ma'am. I couldn't relate to what she must have been going through, so I limited my communications to the people in her office with whom I'd built good relationships. I was not expecting that Ma'am would be thinking about me and my future when she had more pressing issues that needed her attention.

I was surprised to get a call to come and see her at the Union Buildings a few days after her resignation. We spoke about my studies and my experience at SOAS. I was totally perplexed. I kept thinking, 'Ma'am, now is not the time to be worrying about anyone else!' But therein lay one of the many lessons I would learn from her as a leader: to be a piece of secure ground for your people so they can produce their best thinking even in the midst of a crisis. I think my youthful naivete might have taken over, and I blurted out:

'What are you going to do now?' I seemed to be more worried about her than she was.

'You know that I'm a teacher first. I'm going back to the classroom.'

I'd always known that Ma'am had an ear kept wide open for any discussion on education, and that she'd pushed everyone on her team to be engaged in some sort of educational pursuit, but I'd lost sight of the fact that her actual first job was as a teacher. Her plans were already underway for the establishment of the Umlambo Foundation, which would focus on turning around underperforming schools in the most destitute areas of the country. She pulled out a blank piece of paper from a desk drawer, grabbed a pen and started drawing.

'Look. South Africa has a five-quintile school system. Think about it like five buckets to classify the different school systems. Quintile-1 caters for the poorest 20% of learners, with Quintile-5 being the least poor. These distinctions affect school funding and fee structure. Are you following?'

'Yes, Ma'am.'

'In most cases, the lower the quintile, the poorer the performance. We have to look into this and figure out how we can make a difference. We just can't accept that the poorest schools will forever perform poorly. It doesn't have to be that way.'

'But . . . there are a ton of government interventions in those schools already, no?' I was trying to follow her words and the illustration on the sheet of paper between us.

'Yes, there are. But not enough is being done to *empower the principals*. That's where we come in. If principals get leadership training just like top executives do, and are exposed to strategies to drive performance and turn around underperformance, we can break the pattern. Going to school in the townships or a rural area shouldn't mean you are doomed to a subpar teaching and learning experience in an overall underperforming school.'

I nodded more vigorously now.

'Have you heard of Mbilwi Secondary School? They've been producing a 100% pass rate since 1994. It's a maths and science powerhouse. Do you know where it is? Limpopo. You can be a part of normalising Mbilwi.'

I'd never been exposed to an organisation with such a clear mission and an alignment to purpose-driven work: our primary clients would be the school principals of under-resourced and underperforming schools. I didn't know any of these things at the time, but its simplicity made me feel like I was being invited to do something meaningful. I didn't know how and what I was going to contribute to this mission but I was excited by the prospect of being a part of this team. Still, as positively charged as I was, I had a lot of questions. How would we fulfil our mission exactly? What would my role be? Did it make sense for me to leave the presidency for the Umlambo Foundation? I had equal amounts of excitement and trepidation. I'd just completed my master's degree, which was meant to be a stepping stone to a career in the foreign service. All the friends that I had graduated with from the University of Pretoria had gone on to join the Department of Foreign Affairs, as it was then called. I thought I had taken a detour by going to the presidency first and then doing my master's at SOAS, so as far as I could see, the next step from the presidency was to try and to make it into foreign affairs with the unique experience I'd gained. I'd thought that I had it all figured out: I would join one of the regional desks and slowly earn the identity of becoming a diplomat. It was a quick two-step recipe, and I was already on my way. Now, instead, I was pondering whether to accept an invitation to join the Umlambo Foundation team to make a difference in the schools that needed the most help. This would be a completely new venture in every sense. My biggest fear was that I knew nothing about the education system and even less about the leadership challenges of principals in under-resourced and underperforming schools. There was also the fact that I was still employed by the presidency. I was just a lowly staffer, and I was not directly affected by the changes at the top. I could stay and hope that I would have a place within the incoming administration. The choices I made here would determine whether this would be a good luck or a bad luck moment for the rest of my life.

I later read and was influenced by business consultant Jim Collins' book, *Great by Choice*, where he described a 'luck moment' as a pure convergence of events outside of your control that land you in an unexpected position with un-expected choices. The moment itself was not inherently good or bad; it was the choices and decisions to be made from that place that would determine whether it becomes a good luck or a bad luck moment. The outcome, Collins said, was your 'return on luck'.

'I'm in. I want to join the foundation.'

I wasn't under pressure to make the decision there and then, but I did. It felt like the first unshackling of the chains of control that I had placed on myself. I could have played it safe and held on to my job at the presidency and hoped for the best. After all, I had always known that the best thing was always the least risky. And yet, in that moment, my gut was telling me that the best path was the one less travelled. I was being invited to go on a journey with a destination which had not been predetermined but that would emerge with each step. I didn't know it then, but I suspected that what gave me the confidence to loosen the hold on the reins of control was the psychological safety I was being afforded. I could openly ask questions about this opportunity without fear that Ma'am would feel offended by my uncertainty or my need to work through the decisions for myself. To my surprise, it felt exhilarating to be able to step away from the playbook of compliance and decide for myself. Right or wrong, I would soon learn if this would turn into a good or a bad luck moment. What would it be?

'Ma'am, you know that I know nothing about education, or leadership for that matter. I've just come back with a master's in international studies and diplomacy. I can't see what and where I can contribute.'

'We'll fix that.'

And we did.

She spoke and scribbled for a few more minutes. We would work in partnership with the various district offices, looking after the poorest schools in the country. We would enrol participating principals and deputy principals in an Advanced Certificate in Education (ACE) at the University of Johannesburg (UJ). The ACE programme was a relatively new offering from UJ, and a response to the need to build the leadership capability of school principals in the country. On top of the academic foundation the principals would get from their two-year ACE programme, the Umlambo Foundation would add mentorship skills to this, gleaned from established leaders in business, and by so doing transplant leadership insights into the education system. We would also secure donations and sponsorships for select projects from an ecosystem of private sector donors, thereby closing some of the infrastructure gaps in the schools. After all, a principal leading a school with no library, laboratory or computer centre could do only so much. A leader needed an enabling environment in which to lead. Our job was to give every principal the best possible chance to lead for improved results.

I took the leap. I've often wondered how the Reverend Chikane might have captured that day in September 2008 had he been in the room. I remain at a loss for words when I try to describe how, even in the midst of what must have been her biggest crisis, here was a leader already thinking and executing what important work she needed to do next. It was a masterclass in agility and moving with intuition. I've heard a lot of talk about women who lift as they rise. In the moment, the lift was almost a physical feeling. Ma'am had me by the hand and was inviting me to see yet another hidden capability that I didn't know could be developed in me. In that very moment I was moved by the belief being shown in me.

At the end of the conversation, in her signature style, she gave me an assignment. She sent me off to look up the requirements to apply for the Pretoria-Washington exchange programme that might help me close some of my knowledge and experience gaps. There was an opportunity for placement in the mayor's office in Washington, D.C. in a department that coordinated and directed funds donated by business to improve educational outcomes in the district of Maryland. If I got in, I would gain direct experience of working in a government office that was focused on educational outcomes.

I had never heard of this sister-city exchange programme, but soon learnt that the two respective capital cities regularly created opportunities for young professionals to exchange roles and experience structured work opportunities. Although the opportunity was not a direct mirror of the work I would do at the Umlambo Foundation, it was close enough to deepen my understanding of the way business might influence education outcomes and how to leverage corporate social investment for societal impact. The cherry on the top was that I'd get to visit schools, interact with school principals and see for myself how schools and learners thrived when all the stakeholders were involved in the performance outcomes.

I found the contact details for Lafayette Barnes, who would later become a mentor and uncle to me for many years thereafter. Lafayette was the coordinator of the programme, a responsibility that he fulfilled as part of his role in the office of the mayor in the U.S. capital. The exchange programme was more than just part of Lafayette's job. When we set up our first telephone conversation – in which he interviewed me – it felt more like a pitch than an interview. The line carried his energy and enthusiasm, and this infected me. By the end of the call I was on tenterhooks, anxious, and I had my fingers crossed that I'd be considered for this opportunity. My head was spinning. What was I doing? I submitted my application and in a few weeks' time I got the news: I was headed to America.

As I worked on finishing my SOAS dissertation before leaving, I wondered if this was an Icarus moment for my family. Was I going too far? I shared the news with my family with some trepidation, expecting at least some fear, or maybe a hesitant, half-hearted excitement. It was one thing to go to London as a student and quite another to go to the great United States of America as a working woman! I could not have been more wrong! By the next day everyone in our street in Eastwood knew my full itinerary. I could imagine that the family members who had warned against betting on a girl had been fully apprised of the developments. I had only ever known a few people who knew other people who'd been to America. I'd never dared to dream that the mighty America would be a place in which I'd get to work and live.

*   *   *

I arrived in Washington, D.C. the week after Barack Obama moved into the White House.

This journey to the mayor's office in the city, just down the road from the White House on Pennsylvania Avenue, was not planned, and was a definite 'luck moment'.

I had come at a special time in history. January 2009 was blisteringly cold, but also warm with the celebration of the first black family in the White House. Just a week before I had touched down at Dulles International Airport, President Obama and First Lady Michelle Obama had been inaugurated. There was a buzz and excitement coming from the appointment. I felt like I was living in a dream. On Pennsylvania Avenue, the executive office of the mayor was just a 10-minute walk from the White House. Every morning felt surreal. 'Never in a million years,' I repeated to myself often in those moments.

I spent a few months in Washington and in that time I learnt as much as I could from Lafayette and his colleagues. I was meeting with school principals and their teams almost daily, trying to figure out what they believed to be the recipe for effective leadership. I met with business leaders who were invested in education to try and to understand how they justified the link between their investments and the performance of learners in the schools they supported. I met with civil society organisations that delivered the funded programmes in schools. From advanced mathematics to after-care, I was fully immersed in the experience of learning about what made for effective school performance. I arrived not knowing much about how school systems worked and left fluent in pedagogy.

I also left Washington with my body bursting from bronchitis. I had struggled to adapt to the extreme cold and snow conditions so when I got onto the plane back to Johannesburg my body was grateful to escape the cold – yet my mind was bursting with anticipation to apply everything that I'd learnt.

I was ready to join the foundation and felt that I could at least contribute something to the team, yet I didn't expect that Ma'am would put me in charge of overseeing the programmes we were running, communicating with our stakeholders and looking after the administration of our team. Google became my best friend. I learnt how to write proposals and pitch them, how to spend and report on funds, how to project manage both big and small workshops and events. The team was small, so there was no space or time to be precious about job titles. I was formally the general manager, but I was also the secretary of the board. I doubled up as a part-time driver when we went to visit schools and as a graphic designer when we needed to put together beautiful reports for our funders. I learnt how to manage conflict and disagreements, I learnt to let go of the fact that I was younger than everyone I led, and I trusted that I could lead a team and do it well. The learning was steep and the experience invaluable.

The foundation's offices were set up in Sandton, which meant a move from Pretoria to Johannesburg. I'd never really spent time in South Africa's business capital prior to joining the foundation. From the safety of Pretoria, Joburg always seemed like the place where only serious grownups worked. As I was finding my feet at the foundation, I was also settling back in South Africa. I had saved the majority of my stipend from my scholarship from SOAS, and now that I was back on solid ground, I could convert the pounds in my account to rands and put them to use. It was the most money I'd ever had, and certainly more than my family had ever had at any one time.

The first item on my agenda was paying back what I owed to NSFAS. I felt it a responsibility to my country to give back what had been given to me. Because I'd not stayed at the University of Pretoria's residences and I'd done very well in my academic programme, a large part of my debt had been converted into a grant, so I owed just R16 000 for the four-and-a-half years in which I'd finished two degrees. Now that I was debt free, I could show my family that I was a bet that had been worth it. I took the seven-hour bus ride bus from Johannesburg to Pietermaritzburg.

'We're going to extend the house and add a dining room like the rich people in our street.'

My parents and I took a taxi into town and bought the building materials that would show everyone else, too, that their bet had paid off. The mound of plaster and bags of cement were piled at the gate and signalled to everyone that our lives were changing for the better. I don't recall building plans being looked at or approved by the council, but within a few weeks, with local builders from the neighbourhood, our extended house had begun to take shape. There was a lot of fanfare, given that only one room was being added. There was no space to build anything further, but for now it was enough.

My mother bought a large wooden table with six high-backed dining chairs. You'd think that we'd be able to sit at the table for meals, like we saw on TV. Not a chance! The six-seater was only for visitors, together with the crockery and cutlery in the room divider that only came out on special occasions.

After paying for the building supplies, we went straight to the car dealership. We bought what must have been a sixth-hand Renault. It was the newest-looking car we'd ever had, with a central locking system and leather seats! We had left in a taxi and returned, driving French luxury. Our backyard was big enough for the car to fit but what good would it be if no one could see it? The new purchase was parked on the curb in the front of the house. No one could ever dispute that all the education that I'd received had paid off!

I went back to Pretoria with some change. Having taken care of my family, it was time to take care of myself. With my three-months, bank statements from Umlambo Foundation needed for the application, plus the money left from my savings, I put down a deposit for my first rented apartment. I had my own place: with one bedroom, a bathroom, a lounge and a kitchen, this was the biggest space I'd ever had to myself. Over the next few months, I would add couches, side tables and a microwave.

And then finally my first car. I called her Miss Lunar Mist. This was the name of the colour of the car, according to the dealership. It just looked silver to me, but Lunar Mist sounded a lot more sophisticated. It was a Peugeot 207, with a manual gear box and a sleek black interior. I didn't tell my parents; I wanted to surprise them and arrive behind the wheel of my own car! It would become a life-long tradition that my sisters would keep long after my mother's passing. Just a month after the house had been extended, I came home with my big surprise.

'Beep! Beeeep! Beeeeep!'

I started hooting from the corner of the street, long before I got to our house. By the time I pulled up behind the family Renault, neighbours had come out to see what the commotion was. I knew this was exactly what my mother wanted: If I had simply pulled up in the new car, I most certainly would have been asked to drive away and re-enact the grand arrival! As I climbed out of Miss Lunar Mist, the ululations met me at the gate. This moment was not about the car, it was about a dream fulfilled, and a leap of faith realised. My father added his harmony to the joyous ululation while mock fighting in the traditional Zulu dance of *ukugiya*, with a recital of the Mbanjwa clan names.

'*Usenze abantu!*' You have made us people among people.

We were people among people and my mother would subject everyone within ear shot to her humble bragging about what her daughter had achieved.

Back in Johannesburg, I found my feet at Umlambo Foundation. For the next three years I crisscrossed the country meeting with principals and their senior management teams at their schools. I saw first-hand the infrastructure needs of our schools and got back to Johannesburg with clear fundraising pitches that I made to our funders. When the principals travelled to Johannesburg to attend their ACE classes, I led the team in planning the workshops and interventions in programmes that maximised their time away from school and home. At the beginning of each year, I bought newspapers to look for the matric learners in our schools, as if they were my own younger brothers and sisters. The improvement in the results were personal wins and made every day a joy. I was reaping my return on luck in spadefuls!

*   *   *

I've often wondered about this idea of luck, not just with my career, but in how I met my soul sister, Mitch. We shared so many experiences and fate seemed to connect us in many ways. Years after our initial meeting in an auditorium where a hundred students had gathered for our orientation into the Master's in International Studies and Diplomacy programme, she signed my wedding register as a principal witness to my marriage to Rorisang. We'd go through IVF together and fall pregnant at almost the same time. We'd make the ten-hour flight between London and Johannesburg many times over to cement a friendship between our children. We'd work around our schedules to meet in different cities around the world for just another girl's hangout. I would teach her how to wear the *isidwaba*, a traditional Zulu skirt made from cow hide, and she'd taken my hand in the middle of a pride march in Lisbon on one of our holidays in Portugal as we got lost in the frenzy of the parade. For everything that made us different, there was so much that mirrored us back to each other.

My return on luck was a compound one.

What was more meaningful as my river flowed at first hesitantly, becoming more set on its path, stronger, more certain of its direction and where it wanted to go: the transformation of my professional career or meeting amazing people like Mitch and Ma'am? Jim Collins reckoned that 'who luck' was possibly the most lucrative form of any kind of luck. His work reminded me that when you came across people who were destiny-defining, who invested in you, and who believed in you when you couldn't see the fullness of who you could be, then perhaps that was the best luck of all.

EIGHT

Beast in the Building

After three years at the Umlambo Foundation I started to get an itch. It was hard being in Johannesburg, in the heart of Sandton, without becoming curious about the world of business. I had experienced working in government and civil society, but if felt to me that I was missing an opportunity to be in the commercial world. Being in the buzz of Africa's richest square mile had dampened my desire to make my way to the Foreign Affairs Department and the pursuit of a life as a diplomat. Instead, I wanted to be a part of the corporate hubbub.

I hesitantly approached Ma'am. I wasn't sure how she'd take my desire to move on and to try something new. The work of the foundation had exposed me to business leaders. As the principals were absorbing lessons from their business mentors as part of the foundation's programme, I had been listening too and I wanted a piece of that world.

'You have my blessing. How can I help?'

'I'd like to do this myself. I don't want you to call anyone.'

The cutting of the umbilical cord had started. Ma'am had become a safe space for me and now I wanted to prove that I could be a safe space for myself. It was an unconscious plot twist in the drama of my relationship with control. I had yearned for control in every aspect of my life and yet, in that moment, I wanted to stand apart from the support and safety that could lead to a more controlled outcome in my search for my next professional opportunity.

I applied to some of the biggest corporates in Sandton. SAB Miller was a few kilometres away, IBM was in the building behind us, and McKinsey & Company was also not too far from the Umlambo offices. I was overflowing with confidence. I was young, I had a master's degree from an international university, I had worked in the highest office in the land and I worked directly for and with the country's former deputy president. Who wouldn't want me?

My head was already in the clouds. I imagined that I'd find it difficult to pick from all the offers that would come in. Once I'd made my decision, I would move to Johannesburg to be close to work. I would change my wardrobe to look more corporate and maybe I'd even trade in Miss Lunar Mist for a fancier car that would seal my new identity.

'You're not a fit.'

Rejection after rejection came in. Ma'am kept her word and let me fail on my own. I was shocked and embarrassed. Why was no one snatching me up? What was this *fit* that everyone kept talking about? Was an MBA that important? With my tail between my legs, I shared the latest rejection with her.

'You're not going to fit into everybody's box. Your skill-set is not going to make sense for everyone. Keep going.'

I kept at it, sending application after application without being called for interviews. I still had the safety net of a job at the foundation, but my ego was in freefall. Then, just before I hit the ground, came a small glimmer of hope and a break-through. I had met the managing director of Tata Africa as part of a drive to raise funds for the foundation. Managing the relationships with our corporate stakeholders was a big part of my contribution and I had been introduced to Mr. Raman Dhawan on a few occasions when pitching proposals to Tata for the funding of infrastructure gaps in our schools. We had managed to raise a sizeable amount of money in our first year of the foundation's existence, including from Tata, and I was back to ask for more. Our conversation flowed easily from the funding request to my own request. I asked him for a job.

'I don't have a job for you right now, but I think we need someone like you in our team. Come and join us for a month, let's explore where we can best use your expertise, and let's take it from there.'

'Let's take it from there?' This was not how things worked. Time seemed to freeze. My threads of a carefully controlled life were being pulled at the edges. I had put in so much work to get myself out of Pietermaritzburg, to make my way in Pretoria, to find my feet at the presidency and in Washington D.C., and here I was about to take such a big risk. Joining the Umlambo Foundation had already been a massive act of step-ping away from the carefully curated and controlled script of my life. What if this didn't work out? Everyone knew that you didn't leave a job without a firm offer for another one. What if I left the foundation and Mr Dhawan decided that I wasn't a fit at Tata? My ego was also very much in the room. I had been rejected so many times by this point that my pride was nudging me to say yes. I was sitting in my own pool of embarrassment, and this could be my out.

'Nozi?'

Mr Dhawan peered over the top his glasses, waiting for an answer.

I left Umlambo Foundation without the guarantee of a job, without a title, without an offer, but with an invitation to create an opportunity for myself. I had one month. In that moment, I thought Mr Dhawan was crazy and that I was even crazier, but my ego wouldn't let me back away from our mutual insanity. After all, this was the closest thing to a job offer that I had recently received.

In hindsight, it was exactly what I needed. Taking that job was a big step towards embracing uncertainty and loosening the reins of control. I was forced to get to know the business very quickly and to focus on the gaps I could fill. Distinction and making a difference were going to get me the job, not fitting in or being the same.

I discovered that I had very little understanding of the Tata Group. Exposed only to their auto business through the then newly introduced Tata hatchbacks, I was surprised to learn that the company was one of the largest conglomerates in the world. This family business extended beyond cars, with investments in hotels, manufacturing, information communications technology, and even steel. More importantly, I was learning that the Tata Group had been active investors in African markets and the group sprawled across the continent. In that final week of exploration, I set up an appointment with Mr Dhawan.

His office was on the uppermost floor in the three-story building that sat at the junction where Oxford Road became Rivonia Road in Johannesburg. Before the days of sharing location pins, directing clients to the office depended on whether they were approaching from Rivonia or from Oxford, one road with two different names. For the one-month trial period I was given a small desk on the second floor, wedged between the door and HR. I was on the floor that held the nerve centre of the Tata Group in Africa and on that same level sat the chief financial officer, the human resources officer and the head of Tata Power. Their support staff were all one floor below us. The hierarchy was designed into the building and inescapable: the second floor was connected to Mr Dhawan's third storey via a spiralling metal staircase right in the middle of the building. No one went up those stairs unless they were in trouble or had been called for a meeting with Mr Dhawan. You could almost hear a collective gasp if someone ascended the steps to the boss's floor. We would all watch their descent closely, looking for facial clues that would tell us if they'd indeed just been in for a meeting or had been in trouble.

I gripped the cold steel of the handrail and made my way up the stairs. Although Mr Dhawan had always been kind in every conversation we'd had at the foundation, my stomach was knotted with anxiety as I made my way up to his office. This was my one shot. I needed this job, and I needed him to see why he should keep me on his team.

'I think the Tata Group needs to do a better job of telling its story in Africa. I had no idea that the business was so big, and I'm pretty sure I'm not the only one.'

'Go on,' he encouraged.

'I know that I have a natural gift for articulating, packaging and sharing ideas. Working at the presidency, and in particular all the writing briefs I had to deliver, helped me to refine this from a talent into a formidable skill. My work at the foundation introduced the discipline of understanding audiences and pitching the right message, at the right time, to the right audience. I think I can help to tell the Tata story in Africa better than it is being told right now.'

'That's an interesting angle. What would your job title be exactly?' he prodded.

I hadn't thought that I'd have to come up with my own title: 'I can be your manager looking after corporate communications.'

'How does the head of corporate communications and branding for Africa sound?'

It sounded unreal! I had a job, a big job, and I was ready for my corporate experience. I think I might have glided down that spiral staircase with my feet barely touching the steps. I imagine my face must have given away the brilliant news I'd just received to everyone watching. I came out from the wedge between the door and HR and took a bigger desk among all the senior managers in the business. I assumed that this was more than a symbolic play of musical chairs, and that I was joining the team as a contributor in my own right.

I would soon learn my place.

I had been spoilt. Up till that point, every work environment I had encountered had been supportive and enabling: in my final year of high school, I had worked every weekend at Sports Scene, a retail store in the hustle and bustle of the Pietermaritzburg CBD. The hours were long. I was on my feet serving customers, straightening clothes on rails and re-positioning shoes that customers had tried on. As hard as the job was, it felt great to be part of the team. The R1 000 I earned every month was a cherry on the top. There was great cama-raderie between all of us and although the manager ran a tight ship, I felt like I was adding value every weekend that I was on shift. When I was in my third year of university, I started tutoring political science to a small group of first-year students. The size of my group grew week-by-week, and within a month I was given a small lecture hall in which to hold my tutorial classes. The light I saw when a first-year student grasped a concept thrilled me. I was encouraged and sup-ported by the staff in the department to tutor more and to consider joining the team as a junior lecturer after my honours year but I'd left to work at La Pat, the Portuguese restaurant. There, despite the physical exertion of being on my feet for up to 12 hours during my weekend shifts, I took joy in seeing the impact of good service on my pocket. I grew in leaps and bounds. I learnt to upsell, to start conversations, and to know when it was best just to have my service felt without being intrusive towards my customers. I learnt a lot about teamwork, understanding that when I helped other waiters to deliver food and drinks to their tables, it meant more customers for all of us. Later, my experience at the presidency had been empowering and made everything I had learnt in the political science lectures come alive. I worked for a leader who was interested in me and my personal growth and who'd held me accountable to fulfilling my own dreams. And at the Umlambo Foundation I had been trusted to make important decisions. The feeling of being trusted and given the resources to run with my gut was affirming and helped me to learn from my mistakes and my wins. I had no reason to believe that Tata Africa would be any different.

The first time I knew something was wrong was the day I signed my contract. I had left Mr Dhawan's office elated. I had a job! And a damn good one at that! I couldn't wait to get back to my desk and let everyone know. I thanked Mr Dhawan and made my way down to the management floor. As I took the last step to land on the second floor, I bumped into one of the senior manager's personal assistants. Her face was streaked with tears. With bloodshot eyes she looked at me and shook her head. She didn't need to use any words, but I heard her loudly: If you say something, you're going to make it worse.

I looked away, stilted for a moment. What was that all about? I shook it off. Maybe she'd received some bad news. I assumed that because I was new, there'd be no reason for her to tell me the reason for her tears. But a few days later I started to understand the deeper reason and the shake of her head. I'd completely ignored the red flags that had already billowed in front of me.

'You're stupid! If you had more than one fucking braincell, you'd have one too many!' The senior manager's words filled the entire floor and seemed to bounce off the walls, as if they were targeting everyone. The man towered over all of us. His height was intimidating but his words were lethal. This was the world I had just stepped into. The words were not directed at me, but I felt like I was standing in the firing line, as powerlessly as the recipient of the bullying. There was a new victim every day. I wondered if Mr Dhawan could hear these tirades or if the positioning of his office was the perfect ivory tower that protected him from having to confront the beast in his building. Week after week, insults rained down on different people and tears flowed in and out of the bathrooms. And yet none of it was directed at me. Why wasn't anyone saying anything? Why was this guy not being fired?

I would come to learn a lot about the culture of which I was part. In hindsight and with the privilege of distance and perspective, I learnt that high performers got away with bullying their colleagues and subordinates. The real or assumed cover they got from their superiors became a licence to position bullying as if it were a leadership tool to drive better performance. Silence from their superiors and counterparts reinforced their power and emboldened them to keep expanding the net of victims.

I was paralysed. After the third tirade in as many weeks, I mustered up the courage and sought out the views of people that I saw looking equally uncomfortable when these shocking outbursts happened. Surely they, too, felt that something needed to happen in response?

'It is what it is. Leave it alone, Nozi.'

For some reason, I was never at the receiving end of an overt annihilation. The bullying tactics were deployed differently with me. I didn't get direct verbal abuse or a public shaming; instead, I was excluded, and my work was undermined at every turn. As part of the management team I had to prepare reports that would need to be presented to the board. Without fail, every single one of my opportunities to deliver to the board was cancelled at the last minute.

'There are more pressing issues for discussion. Maybe next time.'

I also soon figured out some of the unwritten rules to avoid being bullied. One of them included working a six-day week rather than the normal, legislated five-day week. Nevertheless, over time, commentary about me being an affirmative action appointee became louder. I was the only black woman in the management team and the senior manager would smirk when reminding me that my colour was the value that I brought to the team.

For a long time, I carried an incredible amount of guilt for not standing up to the bullying. But at the time I was afraid and started to walk a tightrope of avoidance, trying to make sure that I had as few interactions as possible with him. I knew in my gut that this wasn't right, but I didn't feel that I had the power to do anything. But what about Mr Dhawan? Why was he allowing this to happen?

'Don't be stupid, Nozi. This guy has been reported several times. He's not going anywhere.'

I was too scared to admit to myself that *if he wasn't going to go, I might have to.* The shouting felt all too familiar. It felt like I was retracing old steps. After only six months I started to feel that I just couldn't stay any longer. And yet, everything I had heard about tenure said that spending anything less than a year at one's place of employment was a bad reflection on your work. I didn't want my CV to be tarnished. Instead, I put my head down, pretended not to see my colleagues' tears, nor feel the occasional prickle of my own. I walked away from the verbal missiles and pretended that I couldn't hear them detonating. I developed a thick skin to being excluded and undermined. I was also too embarrassed to tell Ma'am that I'd made a mistake. I didn't want her to be disappointed in me and so every check-in with her was met with a cheery and enthusiastic response.

'Everything is great! I'm loving it here, and I'm learning so much.'

I was too embarrassed to let anyone in on the silent nightmare I walked into six days of the week. I focused on the perks: more money meant I could trade in Miss Lunar Mist and buy a proper Joburg car. To a minor extent, Miss Kompressori made up for my workplace angst and distress. She was a silver Mercedes Benz and the perfect mask for the hell I was living through.

By then, I knew the expectation. I took to the N3 and drove to Pietermaritzburg to surprise my parents. I didn't expect that my body that had been tightly coiled from carrying the triggers of this new workplace would unfurl on that drive. On the open road, in the stretch between Johannesburg and Harrismith, I suddenly realised that I was passing car after car, driving well over the speed limit. I was racing away from a place of hell and suddenly realised that home had become the safer space. The realisation wrecked me.

Once I had started working in the presidency, my relationship with my parents had started to shift. Perhaps it was the pride they felt because of the big job I had, or because they felt they had done all they could for me as a child, and that they could put down the stick. Our conversations softened and the relationship thawed. I became less fearful. I started to go home more often and I started to be treated like an adult. There were no beatings, there was no shouting. Although these surface changes made for better feelings, and a safer sense when at home, I was still seething with anger and resentment. I also knew that when I left home for the safety of Pretoria, my younger sisters were still walking the tightrope and living through hell. In running away to save myself, I hadn't stood up for them, just as I had not stood up to the bully on the second floor.

Years later, in shared moments over drinks with my sisters, perhaps freed by the warmth of champagne or cider, we'd go back to what happened to us. I was moved to tears listening to my sisters saying that seeing me survive and get out kept them afloat. They looked to everything I'd done and achieved as a blueprint for survival. I was surprised by this resilience, more so by just how my life had set down a pathway of lights marking the way out. I had carried so much guilt thinking that they'd felt abandoned by me – that I had saved myself and left them behind. Over the years, they have released me from this private chastising of myself, a release that set a new and beautiful foundation for a friendship with my siblings I didn't know that I needed.

All of these threads that had been holding my body taut started to unravel. I was ready for this moment, and I floored the accelerator. The road started to become blurry, and when I almost hit a massive truck, only then did I realise that I was crying uncontrollably. I was shocked at this mind-body connection and how I'd endangered myself and others. I pulled over to cry freely and to breathe.

Again, the hooting from the corner, the ululations and praise singing. This time was different, though: a Mercedes Benz was the car of our collective dreams. The neighbours came out too! They danced around the car and prayed for the wheels, the bonnet, the engine and even the windscreen wipers. I handed over the keys so that my father could take it for a turn around the block and for him to be seen driving a Mercedes. For all of my mother's bravado, she'd been too afraid to learn to drive, so she settled in the passenger seat and waved like a queen as my father manoeuvred the car at a deliberately slow pace past the neighbours who had not come out. It was as if I was watching this moment but not quite a part of it. Despite my unresolved anger and resentment, I still wanted to make them proud. Despite the bullying at work, I still wanted the job and I wanted to be seen to be doing well.

The months dragged on. I tried to spend my time out of the office as much as possible. I met with the teams from Tata Motors, from the Taj Hotel, from Tata Consultancy Services, Jaguar Land Rover and Neotel to learn about their offerings in the South African and African markets. I sat with their marketing teams and sales teams and advised on nuances in the local market, how to tweak positioning and language. I managed a busy schedule so that I could be away from what was happening at home base. The territory was so familiar, as if I was back in Pretoria hiding from home in Pietermaritzburg . . . like walking the same path again and again.

Two things happened almost at the same time and their convergence handed me the keys to libertate myself from an imprisoning situation.

The first of these was when a striking woman visited Tata's offices. She was wearing an electric blue suit, walking up the steel staircase to Mr Dhawan's office. I took note of how smartly she was put together as she made her ascent. The hem of her suit just grazed the top of a nine-inch heel, the perfect tailoring, outlining a slim but confident posture, and a blond shimmer of needle-straight shoulder-length hair framed her face. A few moments after the door had closed behind her my phone rang.

'Mr Dhawan would like you to join him for this meeting, Nozipho.'

I had no idea who she was or what this meeting was about.

'Nozipho, this is the editor-in-chief of CNBC Africa, Bronwyn Nielsen.'

Mr Dhawan explained that we were commissioning CNBC
Africa to produce and flight a documentary about the Tata
Group in Africa. I could not have known that this encounter would be the beginning of the end of my time trapped
with the beast in the building.

The second thing to happen was a road block: one of the
senior directors of Tata Sons, the holding company of the
Tata Group, headquartered in India, was flying in to visit the
Africa offices and other company businesses in South Africa.
I knew this was a big deal because, instead of the usual office
driver that did all the pickups from the airport for any visi-
tor, 'an Indian from India' was asked to do the job instead.
The hierarchy in the office did not only distinguish between
the senior and junior, man and woman, black and white; it
included a differentiation between 'real Indians from India'
versus 'South African Indians'. One of our 'Indian people
from India' was a finance manager on a work permit in South
Africa and he was asked to go and receive the director.

'Your fucken people have fucked up everything! Make
yourself useful and go and sort it out! I don't care what you
need to do but you need to get this sorted . . . now!'

Up until this point, the senior second-floor manager had
never spoken to me like this. I'd heard and watched these
expletives being hurled at everyone else in the office, but never
before had they been directed at me. For a split second I
actually thought he might have been talking to someone behind me. With three long strides he cleared up my confusion,

bridged the space between us, and towering over me as I cowered at my desk, he screamed at me to get up and out. I just about pieced together what had happened during the rant: there was a roadblock on the highway just outside the airport. The finance manager had successfully picked up the director, but they had been stopped at the roadblock. When the metro police officer had asked for a driver's licence, none was available to be produced. The officer had proceeded to put both driver and passenger in the back of the police van, with the intention of having the car impounded and the two passengers delivered to the nearest police station. My job was to intervene and make sure that the two were released.

'This is your chance to earn your salary. If you can't do this, I have no idea why we still keep you.'

I'm not sure why I got up and drove to the airport. I think a part of me felt for the finance manager. He had been a friend, and if there was any way I could help him, I would. But I think the more honest answer was that I had been so undermined and excluded that even in that horrific moment I believed I could finally prove my worth. I found the roadblock without too much trouble by following the route from the airport's arrivals hub towards the office. I walked up to one of the officers and pleaded my case.

'I need your help. If you don't release these guys I'm going to lose my job. I can't afford for that to happen; my family is depending on me. Please.'

I don't know whether the officer saw desperation in my eyes or whether he just felt sad for me. I was fully expecting that he would ask for a bribe and, to be honest, I was prepared to pay one if need be. He didn't. He opened the back of the van and handed over the car keys.

Our two cars followed each other away from the road-block and back to the office. I cried the whole way. I felt like the police officer had seen my shame and how low I was stooping to stay employed. He pitied me and I felt it fully.

I went straight to my desk and typed out my resignation letter. By then, I was already in email communication with the woman whom I had met in Mr Dhawan's office, Bronwyn Nielsen. I ignored the fanfare of the retelling of the story that was happening all around me. I didn't care for the animated blow-by-blow account of what had happened. I had been dealt *my final blow* and I knew it was time to leave. It had been 18 months of surviving.

Just occasionally have I thought back to this man who believed that he ruled Tata's second floor, the misery he caused, and how he damaged the culture of the company. I've refused to allow him to stay long in my thoughts – but I've also challenged myself. Why didn't I do more? Why was I not more empathetic to my colleagues? What barriers prevented us all from uniting to quash this office thug? I've learnt with time that bystanders are often paralysed into inaction, held by the tension of feeling empathy for the victim and fear for their own safety. The bystander's fear of the repercussions of intervening plays to the bully's power. I chalked down my own paralysis to feeling the weight of my inability to act. Power-lessness is the opposite extreme to control. I was in complete freefall during the 18 months I spent there.

It was this reflection that created space for me to concede that not all control was bad. Control had nuance and texture, and I'm still learning when I need to hold it close and when I need to let it go.

*　*　*

Many years later I'd find myself in a lecture hall with 40 women from around the world as a student at Harvard Business School. The lecturer posed a simple question to trigger a class debate.

'What do you do when your top performer is toxic to the culture you're building?'

The debate raged. Some called for immediate dismal, while others called for remedial action. In my notes I had scribbled more questions than answers. If I was in Mr Dhawan's shoes, what would I have done? Was there more to the ivory tower than I had realised?

As I was preparing to exit the business, Mr Dhawan was retiring. While serving out my two-months' notice, a new managing director, Thami Mbele, took over. The first thing he changed was the ivory tower. The third floor became a large boardroom and a cluster of smaller meeting rooms for everyone to use. He set up his office with the team on the second floor. I never heard a missile detonate in those last two months, I never heard a tirade, and the flow of the silent tears ended.

A quick LinkedIn search shows that the bully is still with the company.

NINE

A World beyond Markets

When Mr Dhawan had called me into his office months earlier to meet Bronwyn Neilsen from CNBC Africa, I could not have known what a pivotal encounter that would be and how it would influence the events in my future. I'd never watched CNBC Africa before. I knew nothing about trades or the stock markets. I'd had no reason to follow financial market news before and I had not grown up in a family that discussed business news at the dinner table. That would soon change completely.

* * *

In the year 2000 *The Economist* released their May edition with the title: *The Hopeless Continent* . . . a picture of a woman soldier bursting out of an outline of the African continent on its cover.

Eleven years later, *The Economist* was changing its tune. In December 2011, the cover pictured a young boy flying a colourful kite in the shape of Africa, with the headline *Africa Rising*. The investment world had turned its gaze to Africa and the 'hopeless continent' was now looking ripe for opportunities to maximise returns. From a youthful population and favourable political reforms, to increased economic diversification, Africa was holding the investment spotlight.

Tata wanted to take advantage of this change in perception and to position itself as a partner where new investors would feel safe: a business collaborator that already understood the African business landscape. With a 50-year head start, the Tata Group was well poised to tell this story and wanted a documentary that would do just this.

Several months earlier, before my departure and when Mr Dhawan had introduced me to Bronwyn Nielsen, it was with this project in mind. As the head of corporate communications and branding, the assignment of making the documentary would require me to travel with a CNBC Africa production crew to the various locations of Tata businesses and investments on the continent. My job would be to guide the crew as they set out to capture and tell the story of how Tata had invested in Africa for the past 50 years. The timing of this mission could not have been better. At the end of the journey, we must have produced a documentary that could be flighted on CNBC Africa, targeting investors looking for strong returns in Africa and positioning the Tata Group as the ideal partner with which to achieve this. I was excited to be doing such important work and, even more, thrilled that

I would get a chance to see more of Africa than I'd been exposed to at the presidency.

We started with the car and truck dealerships in South Africa, then made our way to the Taj Hotel in Cape Town before journeying onward to Lake Magadi in Kenya. We visited the Magadi Soda Ash factory on the edge of the Great Rift Valley in East Africa. We interviewed workers who shared stories about their experiences at the largest soda ash factory on the continent. The crew and I were in awe as we were exposed to the incredible model of the Tata Group's corporate social investment in that community: it was one thing to read about this in annual reports, but quite another to see it for oneself. Generous and dignified housing, a fully equipped hospital, world-class schools, all built around the soda ash factory – it felt good to be showing investors what it looked like to contribute meaningfully to the communities within which the entity operated.

From Kenya, a short three-hour flight was all it took to get to Ndola in Zambia, where the first African office of the Tata Group was located. Zambia was rich with history for us to harvest. The Tata Group was a significant source of employment-creation in the Zambian economy, including in the manufacture of trucks, buses and bicycles. We met with partners like John Deere and learnt how these strategic engagements were revolutionising agriculture in Nigeria and other parts of Africa.

At the end of our multi-country adventure, we arrived back in South Africa and handed over the footage to the producers, who then put together a documentary that would be flighted a few weeks later.

I had not realised at the time that this would be the experience to pave the way for me to leave Tata Africa and step into my next career.

I'm told that my mother gathered all the neighbours and subjected them to watching the almost two-hour documentary, all because I'd told her of my screen appearance in the last 15 seconds. The team had thought it a good idea for an African voice to add a soundbite about the impact and future of the Tata brand in Africa. This was my big television moment and, of course, my mother was not going to miss it!

I'd not seen or interacted with Bronwyn Nielsen since that initial meeting in Mr Dhawan's office. I was definitely not expecting to get a call from her after the documentary flighted, inviting me to join her team as an anchor on CNBC Africa. I protested, reminding her that I knew nothing about trades, financial markets or stocks and, more importantly, I'd never done any television work.

'Just come in for a screen test and let's see if all your protests hold up.'

The screen test meant going into the studio and simulating a live interview with a mock guest. I was petrified. I didn't know what to wear – what would be considered television appropriate?

When I arrived, there were more cameras than I was expecting and a room called the Master Control Room (MCR), which was filled with screens and monitors picking up different angles of the studio. There was no place to hide. I didn't know where to look or if I would have auto cue as I'd seen in the movies and, if I did, how would that work?

The floor manager walked over and assured me that everything would be fine. My earpiece was fitted and the voice of the producer in the MCR started counting me down. My mock guest was the minister of finance and the interview was focused on the recently delivered budget speech. Thankfully, this was stuff I actually knew about and understood. Having studied political science and having worked in the presidency, I had a solid understanding of how government budgets worked and how they related to the development aspirations of a country. I was in flow.

I later learnt that the screen test was also used to determine whether I translated well on camera . . . I had learnt how to be and sound confident and to hold my poise and posture from the best. The women in the Private Office of the Deputy President had prepared me for this moment.

The letter of offer arrived in my inbox when I was still being held ransom by my own fears. Despite toxic experiences, I had been surviving on the second floor at Tata and had not wanted to leave too soon. More importantly, what CNBC Africa was offering was about half of what I was earning at Tata.

At the time, I played out the scenarios in my head for hours on end. If I returned Miss Kompressori to the dealership to reduce my living expenses, what would people say? After all that fanfare, how would my parents survive the embarrassment of my no longer driving a Mercedes Benz? Maybe if I just moved into a cheaper place, I could keep the car and take the new job? But after the incident at the roadblock, all the questions ceased to matter. My decision was made.

I joined the CNBC Africa team two months later, elated that I was now starting a new adventure.

When I arrived, however, it wasn't to the warmest reception. Bronwyn had fought tooth and nail to convince the head of programming and his team that I had something to offer in the newsroom and could be an asset to the channel's mission to tell the African business story to the world. What I didn't anticipate was the pushback and the blatant antagonism from him. There was an unhidden irritation that Bronwyn had brought in someone who knew nothing about the stock market. The tones were not hushed. I could feel and hear the question surrounding me:

'Who the hell does she think she is?' – which, more and more, was a question that I was being pushed to answer.

I made a decision: I was not going to be pushed out. Bronwyn had done everything she could and pushed down the door to get me in. Now I had to earn and own my seat and make myself an asset.

I learned as if my life depended on it. Fastidiously and religiously, I read all the business papers and the business sections of every daily newspaper. Online I studied the competition and compared notes, from Bloomberg to Business Day TV, and I learnt at a rapid pace. I also knew that there was truth to the scepticism: after all, I wasn't a journalist, and I didn't have the requisite background to legitimise my place. Still, my mother's words rang daily in my ears:

'*Asihlulwa ilutho thina! Umsebenzi asiwusabi*,' I come from a people that are not easily defeated, and we can outwork anyone. And I did.

In the meantime, I had to work with what I had. I landed in the non-market shows and took on a programme called *Beyond Markets* and another called *Invest Africa*. I soon realised I had a unique point of view. Many of the anchors couldn't speak confidently to issues that were 'beyond markets', and the political economy was a scary place for them. It wasn't that the shows rooted in the political economy were soft or easy; it was that they needed a person who had a good grasp of markets *and* the world beyond markets. Bronwyn had seen it way before even I had.

I also got an unexpected boost. I found Karima Brown at CNBC Africa when I arrived. She owned the political economy conversation on screen and she was also editor-in-chief for *Forbes Africa*. She didn't carry herself as if she was taking on less valuable work. Never! She was a volcanic burst of energy, and I fed off it. When I wasn't sure, I'd channel my inner Karima and the confidence would pour back in. I was still worried about my poor grasp of financial market issues, so I decided to do something about it. I applied for an MPhil in Development Finance at Stellenbosch Business School. Over two years, I covered every angle on finance: project finance, banking finance, infrastructure finance, environmental finance – and everything in between. It was like learning a new language. I could now connect the company results that would form the basis of interviews with CEOs to the role of business in financing development. It made for

fuller and richer conversations that challenged my guests beyond the bottom line and opened up the conversation to a
broader engagement on shareholder value and the role of
business as a citizen in society.

I didn't see my own value when I arrived at CNBC Africa,
even losing sight of my worth because others questioned it.
Bronwyn was a reminder that the answer to, 'Who the hell
does she think she is?' resides within me. Now, armed with
market knowledge and a formidable grasp of politics and
development, I owned that duality. I could interview a CEO
about their financial results and after the ad break speak to
a minister about policy reform. When the former president
of the African Development Bank, Donald Kaberuka, came
into studio, I was entrusted with holding that conversation
with the depth and breadth it demanded. When Africa's heads
of state descended onto Washington, D.C. for the Africa Investment Summit hosted by the U.S. president, I flew with
the crew to moderate the conversations for CNBC Africa.

CNBC Africa would prove to be a critical training ground for
the work that I would go on to do as a conversation strategist. The learning was steep – dizzying at times. I was coming off a low base in some respects even as I held a natural
advantage in others. Undoubtedly, the most important skill
I developed was how to take in vast amounts of information,
to quickly crystallise it, and to play it back in simple language
that connected with the hearts and minds of people. I still
lean on this ability heavily in my work today.

I also received a lot of support from the owners of CNBC

Africa, especially Rakesh Wahi, who made it his business to know each and every one of the people on the programming floor. His help even went as far as offering my sister a job as a receptionist at *Forbes Africa* when I approached him in distress about her fruitless job search. His generosity meant so much to me. He might have thought he was just offering her a job, but we knew that he was offering her an escape out of home. I could rest easy when all my sisters were out of the house and everyone was safe.

After work each day, coming out of the CNBC Africa newsroom, thanks to the support of Bronwyn, Karima and Rakesh, *I knew exactly who I was.*

TEN

Who the Hell
does She think She is?

For a river to meander, water must twist and turn around whatever obstruction it encounters – boulders, mountains, land. For me, some of these boulders and mountains were within me, at other times it was in my environment; sometimes in my own family. At CNBC, it felt as if my river could flow more freely. It was time to start doing the work I'd not been in a position to do before – to know myself and, importantly, to begin to understand my mother.

* * *

Over the course of my life, often during my time at CNBC, and certainly after that, I had a front row seat to some of the most profound leaders in the world and the wisest and brightest minds. I have met or interviewed my fair share of powerful women, including President Ellen Johnson Sirleaf, First

131

Lady Graça Machel, First Lady Zanele Mbeki, the First Lady of Rwanda, Jeanette Kagame, Michelle Obama on the Obamas' first visit to South Africa in 2013, Melinda French Gates when she delivered her peace talk for the Desmond and Leah Tutu Foundation, former head of the International Monetary Fund, Christine Lagarde, and the Crown Princess of Sweden, among many others.

On the occasion that I was called by the president of the International Women's Forum (IWF) of South Africa, Nolitha Fakude, to co-host a celebration of three honorees recognised by the organisation annually for their contribution to society and their work advancing other women, I met the First Lady of Namibia, Her Excellency Monica Geingob. I was struck by her height. She was regal, had a perfect coif that sat like a well-accustomed crown. Her poise forced you to sit up straight before she started speaking, but it was more than just her graceful demeanour that captivated me; it was the substance of what she said:

'When they start to ask, 'Who the hell does she think she is?', then you should know you are doing the right work and moving in the right direction.'

Who the hell does she think she is?

I'd heard the words so many times before. As I listened to Monica Geingob, I realised what had allowed me to finally release the anger and resentment I was carrying for my parents. Therapy and prayer had definitely played a large part of the journey towards forgiveness, but it was only by fully understanding the world my mother had needed to survive in and to see her in *that context* over the years, that I was able to heal.

When my mother learnt of my conviction to go to university despite the fact that nobody in my family had been, she naively and excitedly shared it with her family, expecting her sisters in particular to be overjoyed at the prospect of one of their nieces finally making it through university gates. But, instead, what she was confronted with was smirking and unbridled laughter. 'Who the hell does she think she is?' they asked. Why Nozi, and why now, were the questions they shot at her. She was condescendingly advised of the many safer pathways and professions that I could follow instead of the reckless decision my mother would be making if she supported me. On the list were the usual suspects. I could be a teacher or a nurse and if I wanted to be fancy, a social worker would be enough. There was palpable anger in their words, too. They thought it selfish that I'd put this request to my parents and were convinced I'd hoodwinked them into thinking this was something I could achieve. It was selfish and it needed to be stopped. Stories of people in the community who'd sent their girls to university only for them to return with babies and no degrees were dug up and held as exhibits A to Z. It was also the first time I truly saw sibling rivalry in its full ugliness. I'd always known that among her sisters there was an ongoing rivalry about whose children were doing better or best, but I had honestly never thought it could manifest in this way. I made a vow then always to be on good terms with my siblings so that we could rally around our children instead of using them as weapons against each other.

When my mother shared this story of how her family had responded to the idea of my going to university, it opened a rare window for me to take a closer look at her own childhood. She was a middle child born to a 'kitchen girl' and a petty thief. She had an older sister, two younger sisters and a brother. Gogo worked in the homes of white people as a maid, tending to their households and looking after their children and was therefore mostly always away. I never met my grandfather, but I'm told that he was known for petty theft, which often landed him in jail. In and out of prison, he eventually died while incarcerated. For the most part, my mother and her siblings raised themselves. Asking or stretching for more would have come up against the response: 'Who the hell does she think she is?'

For a middle child, without the blessing and the crown of the eldest, without the sympathy of being the youngest, with an absent father and a mother whose presence was felt only through the money sent for food, going to school was already a stretch. Understandably, then, after completing her tenth year of school – the end of Standard 8, or what she described as Form 3 – my mother pocketed her Junior Certificate (JC) and walked out of the school gate. The JC, as it was referred to then, was designed to meet the needs of the economy and social structure of apartheid South Africa. My mother would have taken subjects like mathematics, science, history, geography, English and Afrikaans, with enormous variances in the quality of the way these subjects were taught between white schools and black schools, as per the codes and the policy of Bantu Education. To receive your JC, you needed to take a set of standardised examinations. For white students it was a doorway to vocational education; for black students, the gateway was to positions of manual labour or similarly un-skilled roles, those seen as fit for blacks. My mother had done all she could with all that she had, and had come to the end of her academic journey.

I've always attributed my mother's entrepreneurial spirit to a healthy dose of having to survive in the context of her circumstances and, perhaps, also learning a thing or three from her father. Her sense of entrepreneurship was key to raising us. She always found a place to set up her makeshift shop outside the factories where my father worked. She'd quickly put up a rudimentary structure, whether a PVC tent salvaged from a sale or corrugated iron sheets from a hard-ware store, so establishing a functional commercial base was never an issue. From these structures she would serve the workers meals as she raised her children. I was reared along-side many cousins who lived with us, and any pictures we had of my mother at work always featured a child with a full belly and a broad smile on an industrial plot in the midst of factory fumes.

Life had not been kind to my mother as a black woman in apartheid South Africa. The world had largely failed her, and she had got as far as she could.

I remember becoming fully conscious of her naked body for the first time when my youngest sister was born. She had just come from the hospital and needed me to help her apply the medication to protect her scar from infection. I had never seen a caesarean scar before, let alone a vertical one. It looked angry and haphazardly stapled together. I couldn't believe that she'd done this four times! I learnt in later years that black women were far more likely to have vertical caesareans than white women. The unequal access to healthcare, resource constraints that favoured vertical cuts so the doctor could access the uterus more quickly, and the inferior training and lesser experience of medical staff allocated to black hospitals, made this type of surgical practice normal for women like my mother.

I only ever knew my mother to be *MakaNozi*, as she was called by everyone. Her identity was designated to her according to who she was within the community, and not according to her. As black women, we start to shed our own identities from the moment the promise of lobola is fulfilled. My mother became *uMakoti wakaMbanjwa* when she and my father chose each other, and then *MakaNozi* when she had me. We lost sight of who she was in her own right. It had never struck me that she'd nurtured different desires or dreams for herself, or that she'd ever thought herself destined to be anything other than what she already was – a mother, a wife and an enabler of all of us.

My mother was big on birthdays, mainly because she'd never been able to celebrate her own. Birthdays were welcomed with the fanfare of a black forest cake from Pick n Pay, a 1.25 litre bottle of your favourite cooldrink and, if funds allowed, maybe a large packet of chips for everyone to share. We loved birthdays! We sang for each other and made sure that the day was made special with the largest piece of cake for the birthday girl or boy. Presents were never part of the celebrations, just family and a good time.

It came as a shock to all of us when, on her 48th birthday, my mother announced that she wanted to go back to school. She was clear in her conviction. She told our shocked faces, some with large eyes, others squinted with confusion, that she wanted to go back so that she could become a professional. She said she didn't want to die without having assumed the true identity of who s*he believed she was meant to be*. She wanted to be a teacher and, starting from the year in which she turned 48, she was going to work to make that happen. We all thought she'd lost her mind.

When I reflect on the fact that I'm writing this book eight years younger than she was at the time of this announcement, it strikes me how young she still was, but also how old she must have appeared in my child's eyes to be making this bold declaration about returning to school. She had a clear plan. She'd go to night school and participate in the government's Adult Basic Education programme or, more commonly, ABET. She would do grades 11 and 12, becoming a matriculant at the age of 50.

At this time, I had just left for university and couldn't quite wrap my head around what was happening with my mother, and what was triggering this journey that she was so intent on embarking upon. My mother had become like a dog with a bone! There is an age-old joke in Zulu culture that people who came from the Mkhize clan were known for their quick temper and an ability to back up that fury with quick action.

They didn't back down from fights. My mother lived up to her maiden name in every sense. I'd seen how she'd fight to get us into schools, or for medical attention in a crowded clinic, and even for municipal services when our lights were cut off. Now I was seeing her fighting for herself.

She not only finished grades 11 and 12 in the two years as she'd planned, but went on to register for a Bachelor of Education degree at the University of South Africa (UNISA). She sat at her vendor's table, and later in her Albany container, with her textbooks and study guides, and between serving customers, my mother made time to study and occasionally meet up with her study group composed of the other women she'd found registered for the same degree.

It was not easy going for her and her study group. I remember being cajoled to drive five hours from Pretoria to Pietermaritzburg to come and teach the group about mitochondria. They were struggling with the complexity of biology, and their comparatively poor collective grasp of English meant the textbooks were near-incomprehensible. By then, I had extended our home, and the prized wooden dining table became the gathering place for her and her friends as they struggled through the university curriculum. It was at that table that I explained the double-membrane structure of mitochondria to a group of 50-year-olds on a mission to become who they'd always believed they were destined to be.

My mother completed her university degree in record time and graduated the year she turned 53. One of my favourite pictures in my home today is of the crocodile smiles that my mother, my dad and I sported on the day of her graduation. I could not have been prouder. I could not believe that my mother had achieved her destiny and embodied her lost identity. My mother, the graduate, then applied for a teaching post and became a teacher at Eastwood Primary School at the age of 53. She definitely knew who the hell she was!

That picture holds a special place in my heart. I now know that this was also the day that my future husband fell in love with me.

ELEVEN

A Forever Home

I first met Rori at the CNBC Africa studios.

I was doing a show with the veteran journalist, Godfrey Mutizwa, profiling young political leaders in South Africa ahead of the national elections in 2014. We had a live audience of at least 60 young comrades who were eager to hear from the panel of representatives from the African National Congress, the Economic Freedom Fighters, the Inkatha Freedom Party and Agang – the party represented by this man named Rory. The producer spoke to us via our earpieces, telling Godfrey that a guest was running late. All the panellists were accounted for, except Rory from Agang.

'Hold for 30 seconds. Rory is here.'

Who was this guy delaying a live broadcast with an in-studio audience? I expected a white man to join us – all the Rory's I knew were white. *Which black family would name their child Rory?* To my surprise, a lanky young black guy sauntered into the studio: Rorisang Tshabalala. Rori, then.

We were immersed in the 60-minute live conversation, led largely by Godfrey, with my role being to integrate the views of the audience into the debate. We went through each of their party manifestos and interrogated them through a robust debate during the hour. At the end of the broadcast, we thanked our audience and our panellists, and I made a beeline for the EFF's Mbuyiseni Ndlozi. I wanted him to help me get his Commander in Chief, Julius Malema, onto the show. Rori left the studio while I was pursuing Mbuyiseni, and we would not see each other again for at least another year-and-a-half.

In late 2015 we met again as fellow participants in the African Leadership Initiatives (ALI) Youth Programme, YALI. Started by Isaac Shongwe, the fellowship programme attracted achievers in their early 20s to mid-30s, and over seminars spread across a year the text-based approach served as a personal confrontation where each fellow could consider how they were contributing to the betterment of society.

Rori had just come out of the election experience in which Agang had disappointed at the polls and I was still finding my feet, and voice, at CNBC Africa. The fellowship was taking place on the Spier Wine Estate in Stellenbosch. We were in the lap of luxury and were treated to the best possible hospitality. This certainly wasn't my everyday environment, and I was grateful to be there.

Rori and I didn't warm to each other immediately. He said that I had a chip on my shoulder and was annoyed at the fact that I didn't remember him from the debate the year before.

In my defence, I had interviewed hundreds of people that year and unless they were making outlandish claims that drew attention, I was unlikely to remember every face and every guest. We stayed clear of each other as much as we could. I didn't like his attitude and he liked mine even less.

At the end of the first week of the fellowship we were invited to share our reflections on the experience up till that point. Rori had hardly contributed to the discussions for most of the week, while the rest of us were like jumping jacks all eager to have our voices heard. When he was called on to share his reflections, he slumped in his chair and said:

'People who are changing the world are not sitting on wine farms pontificating about what needs to be done. They are out in the arena with their sleeves rolled up, actually doing the work. It makes me wonder why I'm here.'

This might have been the most profound and powerful reflection of the fellowship – an example of the inner provocation that happened in the programme when participants were truly engaged – but it irked me that it had come from the one guy I didn't like!

Reflecting much later, while most of us were waxing lyrical about how amazing the first week of the fellowship had been – and it certainly had been – Rori was the only one brave enough to articulate the personal tension that had sat with him during the week's sessions.

Back then, it was easy to dismiss what I would ultimately come to appreciate as a wisdom way beyond his years. But in that moment, I thought him cocky and ungrateful.

I remember the exact day and moment I fell in love with Rori.

In the second-last session of the fellowship, we were treated to a dinner with a surprise guest. Unintentionally, I found myself sitting next to Rori, but I was comfortable in the knowledge that the person sitting on my other side was somebody I didn't mind talking to. As the evening progressed, we dug into our fancy meal, courtesy of the restaurant. Rori and I kept largely to the conversations on either side of us or across the table. Our surprise guest speaker finally arrived and proceeded to share a story about the impact and the influence that his grandfather had had on the lives of many South Africans. For the most part, the story was inspirational and moving. His grandfather had been a towering leader in the country. But, every now and then, there were anecdotes that sounded like blatant fibbing, ones that just didn't align with some Googleable, factual information about South Africa. I reached for my phone to verify one of the stories, Googling under the table. That was when I caught the light of Rori's phone and understood that he, too, wasn't buying the narrative and was on his own verification-mission, like me. Seeing that we were both onto our guest, that our search terms were exactly the same, we smiled, then giggled in disbelief. We connected for the first time.

'You're an ass for not believing this guy,' he whispered under his breath.

'If I'm an ass, you're an ass too.'

I couldn't help the shy smile that crept onto my face. The walls came down. Of course, in that moment I had no idea that I was speaking to my future husband, but I knew that I was speaking to somebody who would become a friend. Slowly, I opened myself up to the possibility of getting to know him better. With the cold war over, we sparred in the subsequent discussions of the fellowship, drawn to the different ways in which we saw the world, making time to hang out in Johannesburg later too. Of course, if you ask Rori how we fell in love, he will tell you that the morning after that dinner we'd sat together at breakfast and that I'd asked for his number and pursued him from there. That, of course, is an absolute lie. My version? He pursued me relentlessly and wore me down until I had no choice but to fall hopelessly in love with him!

At the breakfast table, however, I was keen to finish my meal of bacon and eggs, and to get going. My mother was graduating later that day in Durban, and I needed to catch a flight from Cape Town to join her and my father for her milestone. I would later hear from other fellows that Rori followed, hot on my heels, intent on saying goodbye to me at the airport, but missed me by just a few minutes. I landed to a flurry of his messages and well-wishes for my mother's graduation. Our friendship grew and we found countless reasons to spend time together.

At the end of the year-long fellowship journey with its countless meet-ups in Stellenbosch, Derek Thomas, our moderator in the fellowship, asked each of us around the table to share, for the last time, our reflections on the year we'd spent together. The experience had moved us all in profound ways. There were tears, including my own, as I spoke about the impact that the readings and discussions had had on me. Rori's turn came around.

'I know I'm supposed to share a reflection, but I'd rather do something else. I'm petrified, which probably means I should really do it. Nozi, will you go out on a date with me?'

I burst into tears: you could have sworn the guy had proposed! It was just sweet and courageous. I said yes, and from that first date we began our journey towards the rest of our lives. Derek would go on to speak at our wedding six years later and he would share the beginning of our love story with our guests.

Over the course of the next four years Rori and I built an incredible friendship and love. We learnt how to love each other and how to fight each other with love. We pushed each other and backed each other up. We were soldiers in arms. We converged around our shared dreams and got onto the same side of our shared hates. It helped that although we came from different worlds, we were united around most of the important things.

Rori had met my mother just a handful of times before she passed away. Their first encounter was hilarious. One of my younger cousins was hosting an engagement party and I had asked Rori to travel to Pietermaritzburg with me for the celebration. Realising that he could not avoid meeting my parents that weekend, he called for backup: his best friend Khaf made the trip with us. I was deep in my big sister duties on the day of the party but I managed to catch glimpses of Rori awkwardly trying not to look like the boyfriend, lest he be confronted with the 'what are your intentions' question. My mother, ever sharp and intuitive, didn't need me to introduce Rori to her. She just seemed to know.

'*Uzocasha kuze kube nini?*'

Confounded by the isiZulu and the question of when he was planning to come out of hiding, he started visibly sweating, which elicited much laughter from everyone watching this mother and son moment unfold. Another time, unannounced, I got a call from my parents.

'*Siku N3, sijika kubi?*'

'*N3? Nijika niyaphi?*' I was flabbergasted, but pleasantly surprised. Who started a seven-hour drive without first checking if the person they were intending to see was available? My parents were coming to visit! Now that they had a reliable car, life was opening up in layers that had previously remained tightly shut from them. It was such a small act but huge for us as a family. My parents had never had the means to just visit their children, planned or spontaneous. After sharing careful directions, they arrived in less than 30 minutes at my apartment in Morningside. In that short time, I had managed to call Rori, who appeared more confident with his home-ground advantage and offered to take my parents to dinner. They were arriving with a niece and a nephew, and to take full advantage of the 48 hours they were planning to be with me, I invited my sister and a cousin who had recently started working in Johannesburg. One of Rori's love languages was curating experiences for those that he holds dear, so I wasn't too surprised to find him on the phone making bookings for dinner. The dinner venue was a surprise even to me. With the full Mbanjwa and Mkhize clan, we assembled: we needed to travel in convoy in two cars to get to the secret dinner destination. Almost an hour later, we pulled up to Carnivore in Muldersdrift, an all-you-can-eat African dining experience. Known for serving different types of game and South African meat dishes, it could not have been more of a hit!

'*Sidla i-lacosta mfana!*' were my cousin's muffled words with a mouthful of crocodile meat, to rapturous laughter, from all those who caught the joke. It remains a treasured family memory and at the centre of it was Rori arranging a never-to-be-forgotten experience for me and my family.

The last time Rori saw my mother was the last time that I too saw her. Just as I was leaving for the big *Essence Festival* broadcast in Durban, I went in to say goodbye. I held her hand and explained that I would be back tomorrow. She seemed agitated, pointing at the door and grunting. I couldn't quite figure out what she wanted. She wouldn't let me finish my goodbyes without actioning whatever she was asking. I was at a loss. But then I realised that I'd come in with Rori earlier and he'd stepped out to give me a chance to say goodbye. Did she want to see Rori? I called him back and, visibly calmed down, my mother tried to smile. She motioned for both of our hands. She held my and Rori's hands together between her own and nodded. We may never know what Ma meant in that moment but I chose to believe that it was her blessing over us, her approval of her son-in-law to be, and her final wish that we may be and stay together.

Rori was, and continues to be, more curious about the world than I am. I marvelled at his care-free nature and his ability to take risks. I let him lead me to places that challenged my need to always to be safe. We swapped childhood stories and made promises to each other about what we'd take from our upbringings, and what we'd leave behind. We found a church that felt like home for us both, and grew together in Christ. I brought style and flair into our lives and introduced him to seasonal colour palettes for our home. My naturally reined-in posture brought control and management to our household. My thriftiness made sure we lived within our means, but I was also guilty of terrible choices where I'd put a discount ahead of a qualitatively experience. I was fired from booking hotels after finding ourselves in the worst dumps, one too many times because it had been the cheaper option! I also taught him how to dance, to listen for the beat in music. That lesson remains ongoing.

*   *   *

'Babe, a penthouse would be perfect!'

I felt tears threatening to spill. I didn't want a penthouse. Why did he not understand? Rori and I were in the throes of a heated argument. We were faced with the task of choosing where we were going to live. While he saw our lives through the lens of efficiency and practicality, I was being pulled by a force I was struggling to articulate to myself, let alone him. How could I make Rori understand that a house with a yard where our children and dogs would one day chase each other, with sprinklers part of the havoc of play, where we could one day sit and stretch our bodies and our minds into the afternoon sunsets with drinks in hand, was more than just about choosing property? The stalemate was solidifying like concrete drying on a hot day. I had to find a way to make him understand that land, space and dignity had been as tightly coiled in my life as the very DNA that made me.

The places that I have called home have been and continue to be a huge part of the journey of who I am. Our petrol-bombed home was a physical space that marked the end of life as my parents knew it and which set the direction in which the dominoes of my life would fall. Our home before the fires had held the possibility of a life unlived. If we'd not lost it, it would have become the place of all my experiences.

Our home in the car was a moment of inexplicable desperation as much as it reflected my family's innovativeness and our will to survive.

My home with the Andersons told the story of unimaginable kindness and risk, of people who were willing to put their heads on the block so that the lives of the children in their care might be spared. If it came down to it, it might have required one life for another.

I imagine that when we moved into the caravan, my parents didn't have the luxury of looking down on small beginnings. If this was our new starting place, then so be it. From the caravan we moved into our peach house on King-klip Road in Eastwood. Small and cramped, *but ours.*

My father often spoke about how he had loved to garden as a young boy and how he'd accompanied his father to tend to the gardens of his white masters in the suburbs. In that peach house, though we didn't have a lot of space, huddled in the corners of the concrete fencing were mango, paw paw, lemon and a curry leaf tree that had neighbours constantly asking us for leaves that would bring their curries and stews to life. My father spoke about the trees with the pride of a father speaking of his sons and daughters.

'*Umango uthelile!*'

'*Niiwubonile u-paw paw*?'

He allowed himself one more indulgence: he planted bright pink azaleas that spilt over the concrete fence in a burst of beauty, and Baba kept the small patch of grass tightly trimmed. While we heard the hum of lawnmowers in other yards, he picked up a machete and deftly cut the grass at a low angle. We all pitched in. We raked the cut grass and filled the black bags and set them on the pavement for the rubbish collectors to pick up on Monday mornings. Any dirty water from washing clothes or mopping floors, with or without soap, and shavings from vegetables were carefully shared with the flowers to keep them alive. When I returned from London and was able to add an additional room to the house in Eastwood, I knew that while my family appreciated the extra space, the real gift was the extra dignity that came with a larger house. Although that additional room took up what little we had of a garden, the pride of being in a 'big house' far outweighed the loss of the azaleas. We were no longer the poorest in the street, and no one needed to see our bank accounts to know that.

When I was at CNBC Africa, I decided finally to take on the biggest project of my life. In retrospect, I realise that when I knew with clarity what I wanted to do, it was a direct reflection of where I was in the journey of forgiveness with my parents. I'd had time away from home – the source of my pain – to think through, feel through and forgive through my pain. The time spent in therapy helped to acknowledge what had happened, what my parents themselves had gone through growing up under apartheid, and to begin to untangle the threads of why it happened to them. I walked a narrow path of unpacking what traumas my parents had survived and lived through, how those manifested in their parenting, while being able to see more clearly the many gifts that they had given me. Before my mother graduated, I decided that I would buy a piece of land and build a *forever home* for my family.

While I had toyed with the idea of keeping the project a secret, I soon realised that I needed my mother's fight and my father's effort to see this project through. We'd do it together.

Finding the piece of land was not as easy as we'd hoped. When I asked my parents where they thought we could build this house, their answer sent me on a real estate hunt.

'*Sifuna ukuhlala emakhishini.*'

They'd watched both my grandmothers move in and out of white suburbs tending to the homes and families of their employers. Their final act of defiance would be to have a home *in the white suburbs*. The search also revealed to me dreams and aspirations that I never knew they carried, streets they wished they lived in, gardens they found beautiful, and house designs they found interesting.

For my mother: a bedroom for each of their children, a guest toilet and showers in all the bathrooms were a must, a gas stove and a double-door fridge just like the one she had seen on *Generations*. For my father: a garage, a garden for which he could buy a lawnmower and an area to braai over weekends for his family and friends.

We finally found a piece of land in a quiet cul-de-sac in Lincoln Meade that was big enough to carry the size of our collective dream, and I kicked off the job by asking a friend who was an architect to help me pay homage to my parents' dreams.

While the clearing of the land had started and the cement was being poured for the foundation, my mother was still working through her university degree. I could only travel from Johannesburg monthly to check on the progress of the house, so the day-to-day management of the building was borne by my father. He bought himself a hard hat and a reflector vest and oversaw the contractors and the buying of materials. No one was going to waste his child's money! I also learnt that because he was worried about possible theft of materials after the builders left in the evenings, he put his own body on the line and slept on the floor in the unfinished construction site. My mother played her role too: when the municipal officials refused to turn on the water, she knocked on the door of the manager and demanded that he do his job!

I had never seen my mother flinch before, so it was interesting to find her incapable of going to the site to witness the progress of the building as often as I'd imagined she might. She was happy to fight anyone who stood in the way of the building but was reluctant to see the project take shape for herself. It was as if the dream of having her dream house, built by one of her children, was simply too much for her to bear. She held back and only came on-site for big milestones. Never otherwise at a loss for words, she'd stand at the edge of the construction site in complete silence to take in the setting of the foundation, then the walls, the roof and, finally, the doors and windows. It was as if she was in complete disbelief and couldn't quite trust her own eyes as evidence of a dream coming true.

Finally, in May 2017, we were ready to paint and buy furniture. I had completely depleted my savings. I had never been so broke and yet so fulfilled at the same time! I told my parents we would need to delay moving in so as to allow me to raise enough money to buy furniture. They exchanged a shifty look. What was going on?

'Hhayi bo natshontshana! Kwenzenjani?'

Quietly, they had been saving and were now surprising me with a budget that would furnish the entire house: four bedrooms, a lounge, a second lounge, a dining room and a kitchen – they had come to the dream with everything they had too. The house was built and furnished with everything we all had: our pooled blood, sweat and tears!

Over the course of a weekend, we walked into every

furniture and appliance shop in Pietermaritzburg and swiped my parents' card over and over again. On 1 June 2017, we left Eastwood with my mother donating all the old furniture to extended family, save for her precious dining room table and chairs, and we moved into a new life. We had broken the apron strings that had tethered us to experiences and memories in Eastwood. For me, it felt like a final shedding of my impoverished status and stepping fully into privilege. I had already been away from Eastwood for a while, but this moment was also a final detaching of my coloured identity that I'd worn for so many years. Who would I be in the new space?

When I finished building the house in Lincoln Meade, though I was emotionally and financially depleted, I was overflowing with fulfilment. I had finally given my family a home which I believed would enable us to all dream bigger, to live bigger in it. The house would be the safe place that we returned to as we recharged and became re-energised, before launching back into our lives in Johannesburg and elsewhere. I had given it my all and expected nothing in return. Rori and my mother thought otherwise. In late July of 2017, I was duped into a trip to take a new car I'd recently bought for a long drive: Rori had convinced me to drive to Durban with him for a short weekend getaway. We stayed at Derek's beach house and let the sand squeeze between our toes while we walked hand in hand in the humid coastal sun, even on a cold July morning. I was too close to home not to pass by and say hello before returning to Johannesburg. I suggested it as we pried beach sand off our feet that final Sunday morning.

'Yes of course, love, that makes perfect sense.'

As we got close to the house, Rori got a call, which he seemed to be mumbling through.

'Can we make a quick stop in town please?'

'Why?'

'I'll explain later, I just need a quick stop, then we can go home.'

Who did this guy even know in Pietermaritzburg that would warrant us making a quick stop in town? We drove around but never seemed to get to this 'quick stop'. My annoyance was rising steadily.

'Rori.'

'Sorry. I was hoping to pick up something so that I don't arrive empty-handed.'

'Oh no, please don't worry. It'll be a quick in-and-out. I just want to say hello and then we can hit the highway,' I reassured him.

When we pulled up to the house, I didn't quite notice in the moment that Rori was leading the way. He had my hand in his and tugged me to follow him to the backyard.

'Surpriiiiiiiissse!'

It was if the camera in my head was scanning too quickly. Everything was a blur. When focus started to come in, the faces were in the wrong place. My friends from Joburg were in our backyard in Pietermaritzburg, my sisters, my cousins, my aunts and uncles, and my parents were all shouting, surprise!' in unison. I took in the beautiful bright yellow and white décor, the balloons, the white tiffany chairs under a white tent, and everyone was co-ordinated in denim and white outfits.

The effort! But what was going on here? Why was everyone looking at me? It wasn't my birthday. Or had they caught wind of the new car and were celebrating that with me. But, surely, I should be the one shouting 'surprise!' then, no?

I turned to Rori, whose face was beaming with the accomplishment of delivering the guest to be surprised.

'Babe, what's this? My birthday is in March.'

My mom responded to the question I'd put to Rori.

'Uphinde wasenza abantu. Ngalokhu okuncane besifuna uku-kubonisa ukubonga.' You have made us people once again. In this small way we wanted to thank you.

My tears flowed for what felt like days. I cried in gratitude that God had given me the means to do this for my family. I cried for what this home meant for all of us. I cried for my parents and what this moment meant for them. It was more than bricks and mortar; it was a generational break from who we had been to who we could become. Short speeches arose from the gathering of my nearest and dearest. Congratulations, ululations and celebrations. After all the formalities of the speeches, with a generous braai plate balanced on my lap, I started to ask questions. How did this happen? Who planned all this? Rori and my mom. My sisters and friends supported their efforts, but together they had hatched the plan and gifted me with the biggest thank you that will remain forever in my memory.

I watched my mother take to that space like a swan to water: waltzing, preening and prancing, she glided with grace through each room. She fluttered about with decoration ideas, trying this vase or that rug. There was constant chatter from her phone and updates to her sisters and friends. The sunset, the stars, the moon had always been there, but she seemed to take them in anew from her seat on the back porch, specifically designed at an elevation, almost as if she was closer to God.

Little did we know that the waltz would end only two months later in September 2017.

TWELVE

Sometimes

I was barely holding myself up a year after my mother had passed away. I shed over 10 kilograms in the first weeks of her death and remained taut with grief. It was as if my now skeletal structure could not bear to hold up any more than it needed. I threw myself into work, taking on every assignment, every show and moderating opportunity that came my way. My mourning bled into my relationship with Rori, the absence I felt staining so many moments that might otherwise have been happy. Rori stayed and held me through all of it. A huge advocate of therapy, he nudged me towards my first grief counselling sessions and then into many more pathways of healing.

In 2018, while I was still at CNBC Africa, still grieving, Rori nominated me for the Archbishop Tutu Leadership Fellowship. I didn't think I was ready for the fellowship but, more importantly, I didn't think I was good enough for the coveted spot in a class of 20 fellows from all over the continent.

The Arch, as he was fondly known, was best known for his stoic and principled opposition to apartheid, and as a voice taking the fight to the world stage. I would learn in my history classes that while our home was being torched in the political violence of the 1980s, he was at the forefront of drawing international attention to the atrocities of the apartheid regime. A Nobel Peace Prize recipient in 1984, the Nobel Committee would recognise Archbishop Desmond Tutu for: 'his role as a unifying figure in the non-violent campaign to resolve the problem of apartheid in South Africa.'

Building on the leadership blueprint of the Arch, the fellowship had been designed to be a learning process that combined theory, experiential learning and practical assignments to instil ethical and values-based leadership among the fellows. With a limited intake, this was one of the most prestigious leadership development experiences in Africa, and perhaps the world.

Pulling my suitcase up the small flight of stairs towards the white-walled, green-roofed, Dutch-styled building at Mont Fleur, I didn't realise that I was walking into my own personal confrontation; that I would soon have to choose between scenarios in my own life.

* * *

Arriving at Mont Fleur, you could easily have mistaken it for just another conference venue. Relatively small, with a 'home away from home' feel, it was entirely possible to miss one of the most significant places where South Africa's future was negotiated. Nestled against rolling hills and vineyards in the Jonkershoek Valley, Mont Fleur blended into its natural environment. Presented as a 'hidden retreat in the heart of the Stellenbosch winelands', the venue was located amid the fynbos of the region. It took almost an hour after landing at Cape Town International to find the road that wound between vineyards, before arriving at the big wrought-iron gate. Mont Fleur's primary offering was the serenity it provided as a space to think and connect with others in meaningful conversation.

It was here in 1990 that 22 participants were largely determining the political future of South Africa in the Mont Fleur scenarios and I imagined that they, too, must have made their way into the large yet simple conference room with some trepidation. They came from a range of different sectors and included prominent politicians, business leaders and academics. Among them was Cyril Ramaphosa – then secretary general of the African National Congress – who would eventually go on to become the country's deputy president and, finally, president. Roelf Meyer was there too, then a member of the National Party and part of the negotiating team to end apartheid. Trade union leader and prominent ANC member, Jay Naidoo, was in attendance, as was Mamphele Ramphele, a public health activist, medical doctor and former managing director of the World Bank, and Derek Keys – a businessman and former minister of finance, among others.

Mont Fleur was a holding space for them, enabling a series of hard conversations that South Africa needed to have as the country sought to transition from an apartheid state to an inclusive democracy: Who and what did South Africa want to be?

These were not the only conversations that were happening at this critical juncture in South Africa's history. Dozens of forums were set up across the country to create temporary conversational spaces, in different areas of concern, to gather the broadest possible range of stakeholders to develop a new way forward. There were forums focused on education, housing, economic policy, constitutional matters and every facet that would make up the tapestry of South African society. The purpose of the Mont Fleur scenarios was not to present definitive truths, but to stimulate debate about how to shape the next decade for South Africa.

I can only imagine what these conversations must have felt like, reaching across very real and very raw lived experiences at a time when the hurt and pain was still pulsating through the veins of all of those concerned. More than just delivering a series of future scenarios or outlining the potential pathways for the nation, these courageous conversations helped to catalyse a dialogue across political factions. They seeded the national unity that would slowly flourish – despite, at times, also seeming to wither. These conversations modelled the public participation that the democratic process needed if a new South Africa was to be forged. Mont Fleur represents our potential to seek and find each other even in the midst of pain, and to discover our ability as South

Africans to rally around the desired pathways that work for us all.

Almost 30 years later, here I was in this humble conference venue with its hallowed place in South Africa's history. South Africa's own river had moved through the untenable system of apartheid, finally coming up against the impatience of democracy. This place, Mont Fleur, was like a small basin where the river had pooled and momentarily created a moment to pause and reflect on how the river might move from here on.

As I took my seat among 20 other young Africans from across the continent, I was moving in a cloud of inadequacy – feeling unworthy of being there. Although I had spent almost three years at CNBC Africa and had come into my own, I was convinced that the only reason I had been included was because Rori had been popular in his fellowship the year before, and that they'd only invited me because Rori had nominated me. I certainly didn't feel like I belonged among the high-profile leaders, and I didn't feel as if I was among peers. In fact, I felt dwarfed in every sense of the word.

On one side of me sat a young man who had just been appointed as the minister of telecommunications in his war-ravaged country of South Sudan. His job was to connect his nation to the rest of the world and oversee investment into digital infrastructure that would in turn enable other critical infrastructure projects to take off. On the other side of me sat a young Nigerian lady who was on a mission to raise funds in the US capital markets to build hospitals in her country. I was sitting in a class of 30-something-year-old leaders, doing incredibly important things for their countries and for the continent. Although I interviewed ministers and executives every day, and my shows on CNBC Africa reached about 48 million African businesses and homes daily, I felt a very small player at Mont Fleur; someone who had neither earned their place at the table nor the right to speak.

Had I become a poster child for imposter syndrome?

I would later look into the huge amount of work done to understand why women suffer from imposter syndrome: from the early work of Dr Pauline Clance, one of the original researchers who coined the term in 1978, to Dr Suzanne Imes, who refined the earlier work to focus on women in professional and academic settings. Dr Valerie Young added to this scholarship by offering insights into overcoming imposter feelings in her book, *The Secret Thoughts of Successful Women*. I wasn't at all familiar with this work at the time, but I was all too familiar with feeling like a fraud, and I reasoned that, at some point, the organisers would catch onto the mistake they'd made by including me in the fellowship.

When overcome with imposter syndrome, it is not uncommon for women to downplay or even forget their significant achievements. One of the ways that Dr Young suggested women could remedy this was simply by talking about it. Understanding how others see your achievements and contributions can recalibrate the scales and provide a more balanced view of your track record. I thought of this as allowing oneself to be among people who believed in you, who believed on your behalf when you'd lost sight of yourself.

At CNBC Africa I had started taking on assignments beyond the anchor's desk. I was increasingly being deployed to moderate conversations outside the studio. I started to travel to do work as a moderator and not just an anchor. The requests came from all over the continent, including Kenya, Mauritius and Zambia. I spent more and more time away from the cameras and engaged with audiences in live moderated conversations. The CNBC Africa brand unlocked multiple moderating opportunities and I quickly started building a new skillset. When Bronwyn wasn't available to moderate at the International Labour Organization (ILO), she put my name forward and suddenly I was moderating at a global level. The duality of being pulled between anchoring and moderating played itself out daily. As the demand for my services in this new role increased, the less time I could spend in studio anchoring the prime time shows.

As I sat with my false inadequacy at Mont Fleur, I was fully engaged as both a prime-time anchor on the biggest business platform on the continent and a sought-after global moderator. With every conversation in which I participated, I could sense a much stronger pull towards this secondary work. But I didn't think I could give up my duties on the channel; I did not see moderating then as a full-time profession. I straddled the reality of wanting to hold onto the broadcasting role primarily because of the stability of the salary it gave me and yet at the same time I was being pulled by much stronger magnetic forces towards something that was starting to feel like it might be a calling in my life. I was plunged into my own Mont Fleur scenarios. From this basin of reflection and personal confrontation, where would my river flow?

* * *

When the Mont Fleur scenarios concluded in 1992, the participants reported on the four pathways that South Africa could take:

Scenario one, *the Ostrich scenario*, offered no negotiated settlement and the continuation of minority rule.

Scenario two, *the Lame Duck scenario*, painted a future where no settlement would be reached, but progress towards a new government would proceed slowly and ineffectively.

The third scenario, *Icarus*, pointed to the possibility of a rapid transition, but one that would be weighed down by unsustainable economic policies.

The final scenario, *Flight of the Flamingos*, offered the possibility of a successful transition that would lead to inclusive growth and democracy.

What were my scenarios?

I could pull back from my moderating world and build a career as a broadcaster. There were plenty of examples around me of women who had done this successfully. I admired Sierra Leone's Isha Sesay and what she had accomplished at CNN, and I was obsessed with Christiane Amanpour, also on CNN.

Or I could continue to straddle the duality and keep

165

moderating where CNBC Africa would allow me to do this, while keeping my seat as an anchor with the channel. I'd seen Siki Mgabadeli hold down the desk as an anchor and moderate conversations on important stages. Or I could do what I'd never seen being done: build a career and a profession out of moderating strategic conversations in a way that delivered value and impact. While I felt in my gut that there was an art and a science to conversation that I could tap into and build a compelling offering around, I was not as sure-footed about what to do with this visceral feeling.

Back at Mont Fleur, I felt largely disconnected from the conversations around the table. More than anything, I was convinced that while everyone was solving big leadership problems, I was struggling with how to lead myself towards my own purpose. On the very last day at Mont Fleur, a guest speaker whom I had met a few years earlier when I was looking for a job in the private sector and who'd been one of my interviewers at McKinsey, showed up as the final session's facilitator. Rachel Adams was one of the people who'd been the messenger and had shared the disappointing feedback after I'd attended multiple rounds of interviews: I was not a fit at McKinsey, they'd said. I remember being shattered. The last person I'd expected to see at Mont Fleur was Rachel. I also didn't expect that her words on that day would help me make one of the most important decisions of my life. Rachel's intervention would be critical in helping me land on my own, optimal, scenario.

Rachel led us through an exercise where we used our bodies, movement and sound to portray different types of leadership personas. A few of us giggled through it, with some laughs accompanied by naïve eyerolls. I thought the exercise was comical at best, and as she debriefed the exercise I had already checked out mentally. I listened half-heartedly, thinking about drinks after the session and the catchup call with Rori later that evening.

'Conversation is the birthplace of action.'

Somehow, I heard *that*. It felt like time stood still. She said it again.

'Conversation is the birthplace of action.'

There it was. The validation I didn't know that I needed, the permission I didn't know I was seeking. Her words flashed like a green light: step into the world of conversation, and do so fully; answer the call that has been lingering in your heart and mind for so long. My work mattered. In fact, everyone in the room needed impactful conversations that might give visibility to the actions needed, impetus to decisions to be taken and partners that would be crowded in, resources allocated to create the world we were trying to build. My work was an indispensable cog in the task of manifesting better and stronger societies. My work demanded that I leap towards conversations, letting go of the safety of scripts, autocue and studios.

I knew in that moment that I needed to figure out what it would mean to be an architect of impactful conversation. Mont Fleur had come through for me.

I don't think I heard much else. My mind had run back to 2016. Ever the explorer in the relationship, Rori had convinced me to join him on a spontaneous drive to Mpumalanga.

We had no plans and no bookings, just his adventurous spirit leading us as we crossed provincial lines, leaving the concrete of Johannesburg for the deep lushness of Mpumalanga.

'There's a podcast I'd like us to listen to. There's a guy I've just discovered. David Whyte. He's a poet.'

'A poet?'

'Yes, but not in the stuffy poet way. He's actually really cool. He just uses poetry as a device to make sense of the world.'

'Fine, but he better not be boring!'

David Whyte's voice joined us for the rest of the drive. It was in this moment that I was exposed to his work and specifically to his poem, *Sometimes*. With a strong Irish accent, his voice spoke about how we were all confronted by moments that felt like they had been patiently waiting for us. These *'sometimes'* moments refused to be dismissed and demanded that we respond. More than that, sometimes moments disrupted who we thought we were and what we thought we were meant to be doing. They demanded that we stop what we were pursuing and who we were becoming while we were still in pursuit. And if we were brave enough to listen to this incessant knocking, instead of brushing it aside, we could completely rediscover ourselves.

Sometimes has since become a seminal reading in our family. It's given us new language to explain many of the 'sometimes moments' that we've been confronted with, both personally and professionally.

That night at Mont Fleur, while everybody sat around the fire, sharing wine and stories and reflections of how they had been moved, or not, by the day's learnings, I retreated to my room and made a call to Rori.

'I had a sometimes moment.'

'Conversation is the birthplace of action,' I think I may have repeated it a few times with little to no context.

This was one of the many things that I loved about Rori. He was always able to hear the fullness of what I was trying to communicate, even in the snatches of short code that might not have hung together eloquently, which might not always have made sense in the order that the words tumbled from my mouth.

We spoke for hours about why this was landing in my heart the way it was.

With my small yet frightening revelation, I sat a little straighter, a little taller the next day in class. I felt like a different person in the same seat. As if there had been a tectonic shift between the person from the previous day to the person now. As frightening as it was to consider the path that I was choosing for my career from that point, it was exhilarating to feel that I was giving myself a clean slate to become fully immersed in the work of conversations. I recalled other, deeply meaningful words from the Reverend Victoria Safford that 'once you have glimpsed the world as it might be, as it ought to be, as it's going to be, it is impossible to live anymore compliant and complacent as the world is'.

The garments of inadequacy fell off. I leaned into the conversations and claimed my share of voice in all the ensuing discussions. I felt connected to every one of the fellows, realising that they could not have done the amazing things they'd done without the conversations that birthed their actions. As the fellowship unfolded over the next six months, I, too, unfolded into my new awakening and new identity. I had come into the fellowship as a television anchor and I was graduating as a conversation strategist.

My 'sometimes moment' triggered two important actions. The first was registering a business through which I would offer moderating services to my clients as a conversation strategist; the second was to resign from CNBC Africa. I didn't want to reduce my gift to a gig and treat it like a side hustle. I didn't want the duality of a fulltime job and an impatient gift also competing for my full attention. This was a sometimes moment and it demanded that I respond fully.

In the many conversations that followed, Rori helped me refine exactly what it was that I was offering to the world.

'So, tell me again, in the simplest way possible, what do you do?'

'I work with smart people and organisations, helping them to have simple yet impactful conversations to make the world a better place.'

'How?'

'I leverage the science and the art of conversation to take on my client's strategic challenges.'

'So, you're a strategist?'

'Yes, but a different type of strategist.'

'How so?'

'I think one of the most overlooked leadership tools is the ability to create the conditions for an impactful conversation, to be able to start and have strategic conversations that might be fraught with dissent, trade-offs and different perspectives from the different stakeholders. This is how leaders move people towards strategic breakthroughs.'

'Okay. I hear you. So, you're more than a moderator?'

'Exactly. I'm a conversation strategist.'

* * *

Although I had found my life's calling during that time at Mont Fleur, since then it's been a hard slog to differentiate what it means to be a conversation strategist and why conversation is a critical leadership capability.

Internally, leaders are told that they have to build a deep and wide toolbox in order to drive success within their teams and organisations. They must have communication skills to articulate their vision and expectations, actively listen to their teams to build robust feedback mechanisms, have emotional intelligence so that they can manage their own feelings all the while creating safe spaces for others to express theirs, use goal-setting frameworks to forge clear objectives and to measure progress, and be inclusive beyond their own world views. All of these tools are important, but they cannot be fully leveraged when the leader is not able to sheath these in constructive and impactful conversations able to drive change in behaviour and deliver on strategic objectives. Furthermore, one of the most overlooked leadership tools is the ability to start important conversations, to create space for the discussions, to know how to nurture these so that they are generative and impactful, and, most importantly, to measure the conversations so that we are able to see and appreciate the value of conversation as a leadership trait.

Externally, leaders are expected to have a point of view on the development agenda, to unlock resources and capability in advancing that agenda and to participate in the development conversation. Forums have sprung up all over the world to make space for leaders to effect their influence on development using conversations. From the World Economic Forum and the G20 to the Africa CEO Forum, to mention just a few, stakeholders expect leaders to have more than just an interest in the bottom line. They are wanting to hear the leadership voice on issues of sustainability, infrastructure development, gender mainstreaming, job creation and entrepreneurship, among a range of issues that make for stronger societies.

My work is about journeying with my clients to do all of this, and more. Much of this journey is not visible and, unfortunately, we sometimes only understand that which we can see. The market for conversation strategists still needs much support because our work is often mistakingly understood as being the fragmentary slices seen on social media, showing only conferences that are being attended in different parts of the world. Yet conferences are but one type of conversational space and, even then, my clients have more likely already been engaging me for months before the conference in an effort to identify the society-shifting conversations, the voices needed to speak to the strategic mission and the questions that might lead to generative debates and outcomes.

I have worked with governments around the world who leverage conversation strategy in an attempt to sharpen policy formulation and execution so that it is more responsive to the needs and aspirations of citizens. It's been one thing to be called by the office of the president in my own country to come and hold the conversational space for the president's investment drive or to facilitate BRICS conversations as different countries have descended on South Africa to unlock the trade potential of this political grouping. It's been quite another to be called by other governments to support the national conversation in places I'd never ever dreamed of going. It's been humbling to take my seat and be a voice amongst heads of state and to know that my work will shape the conversations of *their gatherings*.

I've worked with international organisations like the World Bank, the International Monetary Fund, the International Labour Organization and many other UN bodies, as clients, helping them to determine how to leverage their respective mandates in an effort to advance development in the world. In the years that I have been working with the World Bank, I've engaged with a range of different teams across this behemoth, including those tasked with unlocking financial instruments to fund energy solutions around the world, with electrification as the catalyst to unlocking economic livelihoods for millions of people. I have worked with teams from the International Finance Corporation looking at the global water crisis and trying to figure out how we can quickly make available private-sector finance to build water infrastructure in order to keep our dams full, hydroelectric power plants churning and bring access to safe drinking water within reach of everyone. I have worked with the International Labour Organization to help its Member States re-imagine what social protection could look like in societies without safety nets – a pressing social concern for millions without gainful employment, for those who are one job away from abysmal poverty or for people who might be employed but are in precarious jobs that pose a hazard to their lives.

I've had the privilege of working with executives in some of the world's leading corporations, like Coca-Cola, to figure out which conversations might lead to empowering five million women entrepreneurs. With the Mastercard Foundation, we evaluated how to invest in young people with entrepreneurial ambitions and how that might change the nature and the shape of African economies, particularly if we could reduce the space between an idea and a product or service within reach.

Closer to home, I've worked with listed entities in South Africa, like Nedbank, to strategise ways in which corporate investment could be better leveraged towards more competitive outcomes by raising literacy and numeracy levels in basic education, thereby enabling every young person to participate meaningfully in the economy. I have had the pleasure and the privilege of clients trusting me over many years, like Investec, who secured my services in order to bring women closer to the conversation of their own wealth creation and wealth transfer, and to do it with confidence and a degree of ownership over their lives.

My work with academic institutions has included the

African Leadership Academy (ALA), started by Fred Swaniker, whom I regard as a brother and who has been exceptionally kind to Rori and me. At the 10-year anniversary of the ALA, I moderated a conversation geared towards insights that might shape the acceleration of the next generation of African entrepreneurs in the coming decade. My work with the University of Cape Town and Agence Française de Développement (AFD) to create the space for a conversation about how to reduce inequality decisively in South Africa is a vital ongoing engagement for both policymakers and practitioners.

I've sat down with individuals whose singular voices have the ability to affect entire societies. At the invitation of the Desmond and Leah Tutu Foundation, I sat in conversation with Melinda French Gates to try to connect her voice to broader conversations relevant to South African women and those on the continent regarding the true meaning of empowerment for women. The outcome of her words was captured across media platforms and became a provocative spur in societies still struggling with gender-based violence and cultural norms that reduce women to children even in their own households. At the invitation of the Graça Machel Trust I worked with the team to create the space to talk unapologetically about the relationship between women and wealth creation.

What is clear to me today is that conversation is a strategic tool for organisations, governments, institutions and individual leaders to bring their voices to the issues that determine the types of society we are building and to illuminate the decisions that need to be made, the partnerships to be anchored and the resources to be allocated. I have never taken my role for granted. It is an incredible privilege to be closely involved in these vital aspects of the world's progress. It is sometimes overwhelming just trying to capture and convey how incredibly blessed and lucky I have been.

The last time I tried to soak it in, I ended up drenched in tears. I was at the World Economic Forum's annual January gathering in the scenic alpine ski and winter-sports capital, Davos, in Switzerland. This was my third or fourth invitation. The first two times I'd travelled as part of the CNBC Africa team with the job of conducting interviews on the rooftop of the main conference building. I think I was so elated to just be there, peacocking with my bright South African scarf, that the fact that I didn't have the right shoes or thermal wear didn't matter. Warmth could wait. On the third occasion, I was invited by one of my UN clients. I was floored to be asked to be there in my own right and for my specific work as a conversation strategist. I'd had a late evening moderating session and missed the bus carrying delegates to different pickup and drop-off points. Walking from the main conference hall to our allocated accommodation I trudged through the snow, with better boots and proper thermal wear this time, and just cried. How had I made it there? My 'sometimes moment' was definitely conceived out of nowhere – a moment that then led me everywhere. It demanded that I stop what I was doing or stop what I was becoming. It made and unmade me. It patiently waited for me. My work as a conversation strategist has been a response to a question that has had no right to go away.

THIRTEEN

Tick, tock

B *ooks before boys because boys bring babies.*
These were the seven B's that, at every opportunity,
all the adults in my life tried to drum into me. Every piece
of guidance and advice from my parents, my aunts, and even
some of my uncles, all came down to this one thing: do not
allow boys to distract you and cause you to have a baby.
Boys were the enemy and babies were evidence of the vic-
tory of the enemy over your life. This bogeyman also doubled
up as the birds-and-the-bees talk. I can't recall a single conversation with either of my parents specifically about sex or
even about my romantic interests. It was only in my adult
years, as the relationship with my mother evolved into a
friendship, that we began to talk openly about boyfriends
and who I was dating. When I got my first period, my mother
summoned one of my older cousins who was living with us
at the time to talk me through how my cycle would work,
and the pros and cons of tampons versus pads. Even without

the talk about sex, I knew that having a baby out of wedlock or as result of a teenage pregnancy was the greatest shame that I could bring upon my family. When I left home for university, it was the one thing that my father said as he dropped my mother and me at the train station, and it was the same thing she emphasised when she left me in Mamelodi. I didn't need to be convinced, though. I'd seen some of my childhood friends and cousins whose academic lives had come to a premature end. Parents could not afford to keep them in school *and* look after their children. A natural trade-off took place. When you became a mother as a teenager, you traded in your life as a student. This was almost always true for girls and almost never true for boys.

When I started working, I also observed young mothers being held back because they'd chosen to have children in their early professional lives. When opportunities to travel arose or interesting assignments were available to be picked, my hand was always up because I did not have to think about anyone other than myself. As a young professional woman, I cherished the independence and freedom that came with not having a child. I lived out of my suitcase, I travelled the world, and the only thing I needed to think about was whether the weather was good where I was headed, and if I had the right clothes. I was also quick to dump any boyfriends who showed discomfort around my independence and freedom. I took the necessary precaution of having an intrauterine device (IUD), more commonly referred to as the loop, fitted and coupled that with protective measures during sexual encounters. I spent most of my twenties fully invested in building my career and deepening and broadening my education. I was keen to learn and hungry to get ahead. That desire for progress at a pace didn't dissipate in my thirties and I was more than happy to take on every travelling and work assignment that came my way. There was not a single man whom I was willing to put before my dreams – certainly not one that was going to give me a baby. I was happy to date guys, but not at the cost of my independence or freedom, and especially not my career. Yet I knew that I wanted a family, and I also knew that that phase of my life had to be timed carefully. But I had also fooled myself into thinking that I could always be in control of when I could start having babies.

With Rori love grew, expanded and deepened, and I started to become increasingly conscious of my biological clock. Even against the backdrop of a tough upbringing, I had carried dreams of what my life could one day be. I looked forward to the day I'd have my own family: a husband, a dog and two kids. I was surprised by how broody I was feeling, especially because I had been the cheerleader for the seven B's for as long as I could remember. But I had done the books and felt that I'd earned my boys and babies stage. The need to be fiercely independent was slowly slipping away, being replaced by the idea of an anchored family with someone I loved and a solid career.

As my 35th birthday approached, I started to panic. Rori seemed to be happy to cruise along in our boyfriend-and-girlfriend flow and didn't seem be showing any signs of wanting to get married. But I had a plan, and that plan did not include being a spinster without children. Although I was aware that I could have my eggs frozen, it had been a momentary flash of a far-fetched idea, and I had not taken any action towards it.

Our relationship started taking strain. I could not understand why this man was not following through with a proposal so we could start building a life and having babies together! On my 35th birthday I arranged an intimate lunch with close friends and my father, who had flown in from Pietermaritzburg for the celebration. I hosted the lunch in a private room in one of my favourite boutique hotels. We had a wonderful meal and washed it down with generous amounts of champagne. It was my first big birthday without my mother, and my family and friends surrounded me in love. Everyone around the table spoke blessings over my life as we went around the table. As the last to speak, I fully expected Rori to seize the moment and propose.

It didn't happen.

The red-eye flight the next morning was a fitting metaphor for my eyes, bloodshot from crying. As soon as the seatbelt light pinged with permission for passengers to use their laptops and other devices, intent to focus on work, I reached into my bag and found a little red box and a note that Rori had written for me and snuck into my laptop bag. Maybe the moment wasn't missed after all! I unfolded a beautiful love letter in his impeccable handwriting, declaring his undying love and commitment to me. With shaky hands, I folded the letter and slid it back into its envelope and opened the red box. All of this was happening while we flew over the Free State, passing over the Drakensberg Mountain range. A pair of earrings! A pair of earrings! I could not believe this guy. I wept again. Over the next few months Rori put up with a sulky and petulant girlfriend. He was not moved by the pressure of my tightly curated childhood dreams. My life as a spinster was clearly creeping up on me.

As my 35th year was ending, Rori announced that he was taking a trip to Burning Man in Black Rock City, Nevada. If there was ever a sign that someone was not ready to get married, this was it! This man had to be dumped. In my view, what he should have been doing was focusing on buying a ring and preparing himself for a hefty lobola, not jetting off to a desert on his own to participate in God-knows-what-happens at Burning Man! Had it not been for our good friend, Ricky Robinson, our relationship might have ended while Rori was in that desert.

I had met Ricky in 2019. He had founded and become the CEO of LRMG, a leading organisation in talent development, talent technology and talent advisory. Bronwyn had connected Ricky and me when he was looking for black female representation to add to the diversity of the LRMG board. We clicked immediately. Our scheduled 45-minute meeting became a 3-hour marathon conversation on transformation in South Africa and how we could accelerate the pace of change at LRMG. I joined the board shortly after that meeting. We became colleagues and, more importantly, close friends. Ricky and Rori hit it off, too, and the three of us formed a tight friendship circle where we could be honest with one another and call one another out if necessary. While Rori was in the desert, I flew to Cape Town to see a client and took the opportunity to see Ricky, too. With a stiff gin and tonic in hand, sitting on his beach apartment balcony looking out at the sea, I moaned and complained to him about Rori. I wanted to be married. Yesterday. But the guy I wanted to marry was out frolicking in the desert in the US.

'Can I be honest with you?'

I took a swig of my drink and let it burn the back of my throat. I kept my eyes on the crashing of the breaking waves, mirroring my frustration. This was not a question I was expecting from Ricky.

'You're projecting. You've put your timeline over both your heads. I know the guy loves you massively, but you're blinded by your own plan.'

I kept my eyes firmly on the ocean. I didn't want Ricky to see the tears welling up. I washed them down with another swig. He kept going.

'So what if he's at Burning Man? You're just not getting your way right now, and you don't like it.'

The tongue-lashing was landed with a lot of love and kindness. Ricky had brought my blind spots into frame. I was projecting my childhood, my need for a tightly managed and controlled life onto Rori. I didn't like the feedback, *but I did hear it*. When Rori got back from Burning Man, I tried my best to snap out of sulking and take on board the feedback I'd received from Ricky.

2019 had been a long and exhausting year professionally. I had travelled extensively and I was looking forward to my last client engagement that December in Kigali. On 2 December, Rori took me to the airport at midnight to drop me off for a 3 am flight, leaving OR Tambo International for Rwanda. After we said our goodbyes, I made my way through security and passport control to wait for the boarding call from the lounge. Landing in Kigali as scheduled at 7 am, and with the expected Rwandan efficiency and friendliness, I cleared customs. I grabbed my bag from the conveyer belt and went to look for my driver. Had my driver been at arrivals as expected, I might not have turned back into the airport to try and connect to the Wi-Fi. As I walked through the doors, I couldn't believe my eyes: Rori!

'What are you doing here?' I was as confused as I was happy to see him.

'I know you've been complaining about it being such a long year, so I thought I'd come and join you and convince you to extend your stay so that we could make a weekend of it and maybe rest together.'

It was signature Rori. Always thoughtful, always considerate, and always creating great experiences for us. We left the airport hand-in-hand; I found the driver and we left for the Serena Hotel. Over the next three days, I focused on my client: Nation Media Group (NMG), the largest independent media house in East and Central Africa. That year NMG was hosting the Kusi Ideas Festival in different venues across Rwanda. I was excited to be part of this annual event bringing together thought leaders, innovators and creatives from across the continent to explore, debate and celebrate new ideas and solutions to Africa's most pressing challenges. The festival was abuzz with energy in a collaborative space. With a co-host, we moderated and directed various conversations over the course of the event. While I was working, I thought Rori was also working remotely and waiting for our impromptu weekend to begin.

On the last day, as my co-host and I closed off the conference at the Intare Conference Arena to an audience of more than 1 000 people and said our goodbyes, the last thing I expected to hear was Rori's voice. He walked onto the stage and, on bended knee, asked for my hand in marriage. The auditorium broke into applause and ululation. Some of the NMG team ran onto the stage and hugged and celebrated with us. I would learn that they'd played a key role in making possible this special moment in our love story. Strangers rushed towards us to rain well-wishes and blessings over our life.

I found out afterwards that while I'd been working, Rori had been planning the proposal, with my client in on it all along! They'd tried on three separate occasions to spring the proposal, but on each occasion I'd messed up their plans by not sticking to the script and not doing what they were expecting of me.

In the car from Ntare to the Serena Hotel we made a few calls to our parents. We were mindful that there were many people taking photos and videos in the midst of the celebration, and we didn't want our families to find out about the proposal on social media. We spent the weekend in Kigali as planned and let the moment settle. Rori and I were getting married!

The proposal could not have been more perfect. It was thoughtful with a great deal of effort and planning but, more importantly, I knew that it had taken everything from Rori to propose in such a public way. Had his earlier attempts been successful, the proposal would have been more private and intimate, and a lot more in his comfort zone. The stage had been the only chance left for him to propose, and with a nudge from some of the NMG team backstage he'd left his comfort zone to declare his love for me.

On landing in South Africa, Rori went to see his parents to start the planning that would lead to the lobola negotiations, a Nguni tradition similar to dowry. A few days later I flew home to Pietermaritzburg to deliver the letter with Rori's family's request to come and pay lobola. This was the beginning of the many moments where I really felt my mother's absence. She would have been elated and everyone within earshot would have known that her daughter was finally getting married. My dad was filled with pride and joy, but he was quick to remind me that I was not to wear my engagement ring until the lobola negotiations had been concluded.

'*Akukho mfazi amalobola engekho!*' There's no wife without lobola!

We were about to enter a very interesting period of balancing our own love story with the story of combining two families, with different cultural backgrounds, with the respect that each of them deserved from us as their children. The first phase of the lobola negotiations was set for the following month, January 2020. I hadn't expected it to be so soon, but once my father received the letter requesting a date for Rori's uncles to come and pay lobola, he unilaterally set a date a few weeks later. To say he was excited about the upcoming process would be a massive understatement. Fresh into the new year, on 5 January 2020, Rori's father and uncles descended onto the Mbanjwa home to come and ask for my hand in marriage. Traditionally, the Tshabalalas would have been expected at the crack of dawn. The delegation of men would have had to stand at the threshold of the bride's home and, from the gate, introduce themselves by acknowledging my homestead and shouting out the clan names from the gate. But given that the Tshabalalas had taken a six-hour road trip from Pretoria, the traditional strings were not as taut. They arrived mid-morning. My sisters and I peered through the kitchen window as the formalities unfolded. I had to remind Rori that, unlike in his culture where women play a lead role in the lobola negotiations, in Zulu culture the negotiations are the sole preserve of men, and that it would have been an insult to my family to have had his aunts join the delegation. This was just one of the many moments that we needed to navigate and make trade-offs and concessions, and show up with understanding and empathy for each other's cultural differences. Rori and I'd hoped that, with the negotiations taking place in January, we might have our *umembeso* (the traditional ceremony of gifting each family with blankets) later that year in September. *Umembeso* follows the conclusion of the lobola and signifies the sealing of the traditional marriage. September would give us a solid eight or nine months to plan and prepare for the ceremony. What we didn't anticipate was that our fathers would emerge out of the negotiations with big grins on their respective faces and declare that they wanted the *umembeso* two months later! We were not prepared for that, and could not talk them out of the date that they'd set. I'm convinced that had women been present and involved, the outcome would have been more measured, and more time would have been allocated to planning!

We started planning in a frenzy, drawing up lists for the gifts of blankets that would be shared between the families, securing suppliers for the lunch that would follow and getting fittings for the traditional wear that was needed to mark the day. As the day approached, our preparations grew more frantic and our nerves more frayed.

'We have decided to take urgent and drastic measures to manage the disease, protect the people of our country and reduce the impact of the virus on our society and on our economy,' a sombre President Cyril Ramaphosa announced live on TV to the nation.

On 15 March 2020, the day of my 36th birthday and exactly one week before the *umembeso*, the World Health Organization declared Covid-19 a global pandemic. After all our frantic but happy preparations, we were hopeful that our ceremony could still go ahead. But, as we learned of the implications for South Africa, we were devastated. President Ramaphosa came onto our screens for one of the many family meetings the country had during the lockdown period and informed the nation that we were in a national state of disaster. One of the restrictions was a limit on gatherings to a maximum of 100 people – and only in an open place so as to limit the transmission of the virus. We had spent two months scrambling to put together this traditional wedding and now we were scrambling to call it off, or at least reduce the number of people who would attend. From 250 people we now needed to communicate that we were limiting attendance to immediate family only. We 'uninvited' friends and extended family, many of whom had already booked flights and accommodation to celebrate with us in Pietermaritzburg. That week in the news there had been a story of a bride who'd been bundled into the back of a police van in her wedding gown because she and her groom had not complied with the lockdown regulations. I did not want to be that bride, and I prayed that we'd stay within the 100-maximum allowed.

On the morning of our *umembeso* some of my aunts, uncles and cousins had arrived, and the house was crammed in every corner. Just my immediate family already accounted for at least 50 guests. The first order of business was for the Tshabalala delegation to come and complete the lobola process, paying the final instalment of the bride price, which would then be followed by the families' exchange of gifts. We had not anticipated so many to arrive for that part of the celebrations, but I could quickly see that many had already gathered to witness our *umembeso*. If there was one thing that I was learning quickly, it was that I was marrying into a very large family. More importantly, I was seeing an outpouring of love for Rori and me which surpassed anything I expected. Very few flights were cancelled, and our friends and families descended in their numbers. We were well over 100 people!

Even while I kept listening for police sirens or signs of a police van, we had a beautiful celebration. I missed my mother bitterly, and I was grateful for my father and the way he hosted the Tshabalalas. My aunts and uncles stood in the gap for me and showed up in every respect. The air was thick with ululation, singing and the dust thrown up by the Zulu dancers who seemed never to tire.

Rori and I hurried back to Johannesburg and settled into our home as the national lockdown commenced. He and his family had honoured me and our family. As far as my family was concerned, all the traditional requirements had been met and we were fully married. We were optimistic that lockdown would soon end. We banked on the 21-day lockdown and believed that by the end of the year we'd have our civil ceremony. We had wanted to get married in a church, I'd wanted to wear a white dress, and this time we would have all our friends and family join us in Johannesburg.

We moved in together with deeply romanticised ideas about living as newlyweds in lockdown with both of us working from home. It was cute. We sat on opposite ends of our dining room table, tapped away at our laptops, stepped away or outside to take calls and gazed lovingly at each other over our screens between meetings. We cooked together and ate most meals together. It was not the honeymoon we'd imagined, but it was special in its own way. The cute feeling lasted less than two weeks.

'I didn't know you speak so much! You are literally talking all day!'

Our shared working space was not sustainable. It was the beginning of the end of our romantic lockdown. Rori set his heart on securing a permit that would allow him to go back to his office so that I could do all the talking – the moderated virtual conversations – that were now needed from home. No one expected the initial 21-day lockdown to be extended and adjusted over time. The most stringent measures came with a level-5 lockdown where the country's borders were closed, travel restrictions put in place and we could leave our homes only for basic necessities like food. The plans we had for our civil ceremony faded fast. We had no control over when we could have this wedding and spent the first two years of our married life traditionally married, yet not recorded officially by Home Affairs. It didn't matter how much I worried or complained, this was a massive moment of not being in control and I could only be present in it. As we settled into the restrictions, we opened ourselves up to the idea of starting a family. Maybe I would walk down the aisle with a pregnant belly, or maybe with our son or daughter as part of our ceremony? It hadn't been our plan, but we were here now and needed to consider every possibility. We buckled down and worked hard on conceiving and expanding our family. Initially, we didn't make much of the fact that cycles came and went without a positive pregnancy test. We wrote it off to stress and ignored all the lockdown pregnancies that were popping up around us. But the ticking of my biological clock got steadily louder. It began to feel like a permanent, shifting shadow that moved into our house and followed us into every room throughout lockdown.

As soon as the restrictions were lifted and gatherings were allowed again, we had our much-awaited civil ceremony in the summer of 2023. It was magical! It was the best party I'd ever been to! Unlike our traditional wedding, this ceremony felt more like ours and less about the protocols of uniting families. By now we'd lived together for two years and the veil of the honeymoon phase had long been lifted. We said our vows against the backdrop of a burst of January blooms at Shepstone Gardens. We hosted our lunch reception in an open Grecian structure with columns of concrete holding up a chandelier of white roses. And when everyone had gone, we were still on the dancefloor – we were the last ones standing with the DJ at 3 am!

We must have put our heads down for no more than three hours, because at 6 am we were up and getting ready to travel to Jericho in the North West province. We were set for another ceremony at the church that had raised Rori and where his father had been preaching for more than 20 years. We arrived to a symphony of tambourines and a full brass band, in true Batswana style. The last of the celebrations concluded at Rori's home, where I was officially welcomed as their *Makoti* – another daughter in the Tshabalala family. We left for our honeymoon shortly after that, completely exhausted but beaming with marital bliss. We had satisfied all the requirements from both families to solemnise our marriage and now we could get back to focusing on our family.

We'd chosen the Maldives for our honeymoon and made the trip from Johannesburg to Male via Doha with great excitement. We snuggled into each other in our seats and spoke about our dreams and all that we'd do together as a family. From Male we jumped onto a sea plane that delivered us across the tranquil turquoise waters to Furaveri Island. We broke our budget, but did everything that the island had to offer. We swam with the sharks and the turtles, snorkelled over the most stunning reefs and spent a lot of time in bed. Our honeymoon was perfectly timed to coincide with a new cycle and another window of opportunity for us to start expanding our family.

It didn't happen. We came back from the Maldives tanned and rested, but we were not pregnant.

FOURTEEN

A New Heaven

'Give it another six months.'

I had suggested that we visit my gynaecologist, just for us to check if anything was wrong. I'd been with this doctor close on a decade and I was confident that he'd point us in the right direction if anything was amiss. He had come highly recommended and had seen me through all my contraceptive plans. I felt safe and comfortable with him. Without any tests, he assured us that we were fine and that we just needed to keep trying. Nothing was wrong, just keep trying:

'Slow down. You need to reduce the stress levels in your lives and give your bodies a chance to do what they are capable of doing.'

I felt deflated by his diagnosis.

Six cycles later, we booked another appointment with him. This time he did an ultrasound and told us that I had small fibroids that he wanted to remove before we considered the next steps. He ordered a myomectomy, a surgical procedure to remove fibroids in the uterus. It wasn't a big deal, he assured us. A quick 45-minute procedure and I'd be out.

We checked into the Mediclinic Sandton on a cold Thursday morning. The nurses went through the admin of checking me in and getting me ready for theatre. The anaesthesiologist came to introduce herself and offered words of reassurance. We hadn't told anyone in the family about this surgery because we thought it would be a quick visit without fanfare. We'd be home by lunchtime.

When I came out of the anaesthesia fog, Rori was at my bedside with a visibly worried face. The 'quick 45 minutes' had turned into almost five-hour marathon surgery as the doctor discovered many more fibroids than what had been visible on the ultrasound. I came back from theatre with a catheter and I was still hooked up to IV drips. There was no going home today, because my body had gone through a lot and the doctor wanted me to be monitored overnight. A day later, I was discharged with instructions to let my body recover for two months and then to return for another consultation.

The recovery was quick and hope was bountiful that we would now be ready to start a family. At the ensuing consultation, the doctor ordered Rori to have his semen tested so that we could get a clearer picture of our health, jointly. The results would be out in a few days, so as we left the practice we scheduled a follow-up appointment where we could go through the results. In the meantime, the doctor asked me to take a hysterosalpingogram, usually referred to as an HSG, administered by the radiology department in the hospital. The procedure must be specifically timed and done at the end of a menstrual period and before ovulation, to avoid interfering with a potential pregnancy. We scheduled the test with the radiology department.

The HSG was basically an X-ray of the uterus, allowing the doctor to see the shape of it and if there were any deviations of concern. The cervix would be opened with a speculum, the same device used for a pap smear. A dark dye would be inserted through a catheter into the uterus through the cervix. The movement of the dye would reveal the shape of the uterus and the openness of the fallopian tubes. The procedure was meant to be quick and could be done in less than 20 minutes.

I wasn't prepared for what happened next. I was taken back to a moment on our honeymoon. In the late afternoon sun, we'd decided to go for our last snorkel. The sun was dipping and the water was glorious. Rori had gone ahead of me and I was slowly losing myself in the mosaic of colour bursting from the reef. In one moment, I was held spellbound by the sight of a shoal of orange and blue fish as they sashayed past me and the next moment the reef disappeared completely and all I could see was a sharp drop into dark nothingness as the water suddenly chilled, almost ominously.

'Stop, please!' I screamed as a horrific pain shot through my abdomen. It felt like my cervix was sealed shut and the doctor was trying to ram the speculum though. I'd been diligent with my annual pap smears, so I was familiar with the discomfort of a speculum, yet I was completely blindsided by this pain. My body started shaking uncontrollably and the test was called off.

I called my gynaecologist and told him what I'd just been through. He was baffled. He insisted that he still needed to get visibility of my uterus and if an HSG couldn't do the job, further surgery would be necessary. This time, he'd put a camera through my navel while I was under general anaesthetic and view my uterus and fallopian tubes that way. At this point I was exasperated – but we still needed the help, the supposed clarity this procedure would provide.

So, I was back in the hospital a few weeks later, being wheeled into theatre again. This time it went smoothly. I was grateful for the feedback that everything checked out. The fibroids had not returned, my fallopian tubes were open, and my uterus was fine. Now we needed to discuss Rori's results.

We walked into the doctor's rooms. It had been three months since Rori had taken his semen test and the results had been sent to the doctor long ago. As we took our seats, he looked distracted and didn't seem to be on top of our case. I reminded him that we were there to get the semen test results back. He couldn't find them. I could feel tears threatening to fall. I had not once thought to question this doctor's approach to my treatment. After ten years, I had become comfortable with everything he'd advised and every test ordered. Now I felt let down and unsupported. The lab could not send the results because too much time had passed and Rori would have to redo the test.

That was it. I was done. I was adamant that we needed to see a doctor who had the time and would take the care that was needed. I was convinced that whatever was going on, we needed more attention than this specialist was offering.

I had questioned the surgeries, but didn't have the knowledge to go beyond speculating whether they had all been necessary. But a new determination propelled me to walk away from a 10-year medical relationship. Little did I realise that we hadn't even scratched the surface regarding the time I'd spend on the surgical table.

I'd heard about fertility clinic, Vitalab, from a few people by this point, but had never thought of it as a place that I'd one day need to visit; it had never crossed my mind. When conversations about proactively freezing eggs had come up, I tuned out. That had nothing to do with me.

A close friend had shared her journey of infertility with me. She and her husband had had multiple losses that thankfully ended with a successful twin pregnancy. She was a champion of Vitalab, speaking highly of the care and support that she and her husband had received along their journey. She encouraged me to make the appointment. Doctor Chris Venter was incredible.

'Please call me Chris. Just Chris.'

He was warm and empathetic from that first consultation in which he walked us through a plan, first to get a sense of what was going on with our bodies and then to outline the options we could exercise. Chris had a way of making us both feel safe. We knew that we had arrived at a place where we could get help. We started off with full sets of blood tests on both of us, and Rori had to redo his semen test. Chris also wanted me back on the examination table for the HSG that had gone horribly wrong the first time. He listened to me replaying my experience and assured me that he would do the test himself, that it would be done in less than 10 minutes and that it would involve some discomfort but no pain. There was a small screen positioned just behind Chris's shoulder and in my direct line of sight. The speculum went in and my cervix opened without incident. I waited anxiously for the pain. It never came. We watched the contrast dye enter the uterus and run through my fallopian tubes. My tubes were open – a good sign. He wasn't happy with the scarring he saw on my uterus. Either the process of removing my fibroids or the surgery to view my uterus through my navel had been done haphazardly and had left scars on my uterus. The scarring meant that the shape of my uterus was not as good as it could be. We wanted to give our baby a fighting chance, and to do that I'd need to undergo surgery to cut out the scarring and prepare the uterus for conception. I cried on the drive back home. I was tired of all these surgical interventions. But I wanted a baby. Post the surgery, Chris ordered two months of recovery before my body would be ready for IVF. It felt that with every step forward we took at least ten steps back.

After the recovery period we were ready for the first step of our IVF journey: the harvesting of my eggs. We knew that the higher the number, the better chance we had of multiple tries, if necessary, provided that the eggs were viable. I had no idea what amounted to a good number of eggs. I went down a rabbit hole of reading and watching TikTok videos of other women telling their stories. I knew it was possible to harvest a dozen eggs, or none at all. I was 38 years old and didn't feel confident that we'd come out at the higher end of the scale.

Everything was done at the fertility clinic. It helped to contain the experience and make it a little more bearable. On the day of our harvesting there were three other couples all hopeful that they'd get a good number. With mild sedation to keep me comfortable, the entire procedure was done in 15 minutes. I was still groggy from the sedation as a nurse stuck a sticker with a happy face on the back of my hand.

'Well done! You have 17 eggs!'

I didn't know much about IVF, but I knew that 17 was a bloody good number! We were elated that we were off to a really strong start and, for the first time in a long time, I felt that our family was finally within reach. Now that we had eggs, they could be fertilised with Rori's sperm to form embryos that might become a healthy pregnancy. My body needed to co-operate, but it was all under control.

Over a period of five days the clinic called every day to give an update on the surviving embryos. Some embryos died on the day of fertilisation, others as the days advanced, with some not making it to the fifth day when they were meant to be frozen. At the end of five days, we'd lost seven embryos, but still had 10 to work with. I thought that meant we could have ten babies. The odds were in our favour! My enthusiasm was soon tempered, though: given my age, it was advisable for us to have our eggs genetically tested so that we could rule out any possibility of transferring an embryo that might not be compatible with life. The older the mother, the higher the probability of incompatibility. We had to make our first big decision: how many embryos would we want to test and how many would we want to freeze without testing? Had we harvested four eggs, these might have been easy questions to answer. We started to feel the weight of the cost of IVF.

From the ten surviving embryos, we tested the six strongest-looking ones and froze the remaining untested four. The results of the genetic tests took only a few days and gave us a much more sober picture of how many embryos we really had. Two of the six came back with genetic abnormalities, meaning that they were incompatible with life. If implanted, these two would have resulted in a miscarriage or a child with severe abnormalities. Just like that, we were down from 17 eggs to four strong embryos. It was sobering, but also liberating. We were sad to see that so many of the eggs and embryos were not viable, but we were equally grateful to have four eggs that we could transplant, optimistically, in the hope of a pregnancy.

Chris wanted to target my natural cycle, meaning that my body would be given the opportunity to ovulate naturally before our embryo would be implanted. To support the natural cycle, I'd be given a battery of injections to administer at home, in my belly, over a period of two weeks. I was petrified of needles. When it was time for the injection, Rori would try to find an upbeat song on his phone to lighten the moment, most times I'd be singing with tears already flowing from the fear of the injection, then I'd toughen up and he'd push the needle into my belly. A bear hug would seal it.

'You're doing great, love.'

My body was pumped full of hormones and ballooned with weight gain as we went through the process. Old demons teetered at the edge of my consciousness as I fought off the feeling of hating my body again. I kept reminding myself that at the end of all this pain would be the miracle of a baby.

As we prepared for the transfer of the embryo, we had to inform Chris whether we were going to transfer a boy or a girl: the genetic test also identified the sex of the embryo. I was very clear that if I had the option of not having a daughter as the first born, I would take it. Given the choice, I didn't want to pass on the burden of responsibility that girls automatically carried for their families, especially first-born daughters. As a first-born daughter myself, I knew the weight of being expected to be a deputy mother, caregiver, cook and cleaner for the family. First-born sons carried the first-born responsibility differently: to be the custodian of the family name, which came only with the burden of procreation. Our decision was made without too much wrestling, and we chose a boy.

On the day of the transfer, we arrived early at the clinic and I was immediately hooked up to an IV drip that would loosen the muscles around my uterus and help my body be receptive to the embryo. We joined a cocoon of three other couples, a single lady, and what appeared to be a couple with their surrogate, all of us praying for the miracle of a successful transfer that morning. Hope and desperation held us all together as we tried to pass the time by swapping the stories we'd walked in with.

'This is our fourth try. We're not giving up; God will make a way.'

'Us? It's our second try. This time feels lucky.'

While the IV dripped silently into my arm, I had to drink as much water as possible. The water made the tubing that would carry the chosen embryo more visible on the ultrasound imaging machine. This way Chris could have more sight of the tubing he was inserting into the uterus and we could see the moment our child entered my body too. Finally, it was time for us to go and get our son. Rori was dressed in surgical scrubs and I was in my wrap-around surgical gown as we walked in together, hand-in-hand, praying as we entered the theatre.

'Lord, in your word you promise that you will never leave me, and you will never forsake me. I need you now more than ever.'

Inside the theatre behind a glass wall there was a lab-like space where the embryos were prepared for transfer by the embryologist. I was settled into the surgical chair, still tethered to my drip, with my legs hoisted into the stirrups. The first step was to ensure that we were implanting our embryo and not somebody else's. On a screen hoisted high on the wall, the embryologist projected an image of what appeared to be a dot in a Petri dish with my surname and date of birth, which I had to confirm. That was our son! Once this was verified, Chris reached for his speculum from the tray of surgical instruments and inserted it into my vagina to access the cervix.

'Breathe, Nozi.'

The nurse assisting Chris stroked my arm from one side

202

and held my hand, while Rori held the other. Close to my ear Rori continued to pray. With my cervix open and ready to receive the embryo, the embryologist walked in with small, measured steps and handed over the tube holding the embryo to Chris. Our eyes were glued to the screen. Rori took out his phone so we could capture this magical moment of transplanting a seed that could become a life.

'Pay careful attention now. If you look closely, you'll see a spark of light. That's your baby leaving the tube and entering your uterus.'

Our shooting star was home. We prayed for conception, that the tiny spark would be kindled and result in a precious pregnancy, the miraculous new life of our son.

As we left the clinic, the nurse reminded us to continue our day as normal and explained that the baby could not fall out of the uterus at any point. I could walk, go to the bathroom and live life as normal. The only thing we needed to do now was wait. In two weeks' time, a blood test would confirm or deny the pregnancy. I fought the impulse to start shopping for a child that we did not know we would have, or to start putting together a nursery that I did not know we would need. Then the call finally came. We were pregnant!

Everything I had heard about the experience of pregnancy didn't pan out. I cursed all the women who spoke of pregnancy as if it were the equivalent of a unicorn frolicking in rainbows. There were no unicorns. No rainbows. I was also pregnant for 10 months, not 9. Who had done the numbers on this? Although I never actually threw up, the constant feeling of nausea never left and it just lingered all day. I wasn't sure why it was called morning sickness when the threat of retching never left me. My skin changed quickly, my face remained the same, but from the neck down my body turned a dark almost navy tone. I hated the smell of people. My nose could sniff out toes, creases in people's necks and armpits that had not been visited by a washcloth. I could not stand to be in a room full of people. I felt as if I carried an unpleasant odour all the time, too, while my cravings betrayed me completely. All I wanted to eat were the things that Rori loved and which I had once hated. I called him in tears from a hotel room in New York.

'Love, I want *skop!*'

I craved sheep's head, grapes and Grapetiser. These were Rori staples that I had always teased him about. My friendship circle saved me. One of my closest friends, Khanyi, was pregnant at the same time with her first child. With a five-month lead, she held my hand and helped me make sense of everything that was happening to me. Khanyi was also my makeup artist, so I got a front row seat watching her struggle through mixing foundation combinations so as to make my face and my neck match and look as close in colour to the other as possible. When my clothes stopped fitting, I transitioned to custom-made preggy-pants and large shirts with kitten heels to stay stage appropriate.

* * *

Much to my frustration, we still didn't have a name for our son on the day I was due to give birth. When Rori lost his paternal grandmother, our friendship was just starting to take root. Although I was at her send-off, I had not met the woman who would influence the name we were to give to our son.

Rori had inherited his grandmother's Xitsonga Bible, and it was one of his most sacred belongings kept in our home. We prayed for God to reveal a name for our son throughout the pregnancy. Of course, as a new mother, I had tons of names that I'd been considering. But Rori was adamant that God would give us a name, and we'd know when He did. With my hospital bag at the door, we sat down to pray for the last time before heading to the hospital before the birth.

'Let's read the word first,' Rori suggested.

He pulled out the Bible he'd inherited and opening it at Revelation 21, where John described a new heaven and a new earth. His grandmother had underlined 'new heaven' twice. We didn't need any convincing. We named our son Tilo-Lerintshwa (a New Heaven) Phakade (Forever) Tshabalala. He was indeed our answered prayer in the form of a new heaven that would be ours forever.

FIFTEEN

To God's Ears

The problem with getting things right the first time around is that it gives you a false sense of control. I believed that I had figured out the formula and now we could rinse and repeat. We had eggs but we didn't have time.

Tilo thrived and became the apple of everyone's eye. We celebrated every small milestone. I simply couldn't believe the blessing he was to us. But though I'd desperately wanted to be a mother, now that I was, I was struggling to find my balance. People talked about finding their sea legs to describe the experience of learning to walk calmly and steadily on a tossing ship. I had to find my mom legs. The daily trade-off between being present for my son and being present for my work took its toll. I recalled all the platitudes about how it took a village to raise a child and sought out that village. The village turned out to be very far away, and not really a village – more like a hamlet. All of my friends were working moms, working through their own mom-guilt, and tight-roping their own work–life balance. Life in the northern suburbs of Johannesburg wasn't configured to uphold the promise of the village, so we built our own: a full-time nanny, a night nurse, a cleaner and a gardener came in like a moat to secure our village. Occasional visits from Tilo's grandparents bolstered the support we needed as a family. When he turned one, we added playschool, library visits and playdates to the village activities. In my own quiet moments, I still felt guilty every time I packed a suitcase.

'Why don't you travel with him?'

'Why are you not breastfeeding?'

'Who's looking after him when you're not there?'

And then my favourite question: 'Do you even know your son?'

Thankfully, I was prepared for these conversations. Rori and I had had many hard discussions about the nature of our work and what it meant for the kind of parents we were. We are two entrepreneurs, building and running our respective businesses. Without the village we'd built, we would not have been able to run our businesses in the way we needed to. We also had to get comfortable with the fact that people did not see us at home and in our parenting roles. In my world, people mostly saw my work away from home and had little knowledge of what I was doing when I was not travelling. In the midst of finding our sea legs as Tilo's parents, we found time to dream about Tilo's sibling. We didn't want to wait too long. My pregnancy with Tilo had not been smooth sailing. Now, at 39, I knew I would be classified as a geriatric maternity patient and would have to take special precautions.

So it was that a year later, as we planned Tilo's first birthday and my fortieth, that we also planned to go back to see Dr Chris Venter. We had the recipe, we knew what to do, what to expect, and we knew the reward. We still had three genetically strong embryos. Two girls and a boy. We walked into the consultation with confidence and a readiness to start the process again.

'So, which gender are we transferring this time?' Chris asked.

'Let's go pink!'

A sister for Tilo and a daughter for us. It could not be more perfect. Chris walked us through the plan again. Rinse and repeat. We went through our routine, the injections, the tears, the weight gain, and then the hope. Through it all, we were held up by the knowledge that it would all be worth it in the end. We joined a new cluster of possible parents on the day of the transfer and we all hooked up to our IV drips. This cluster of parents was a little quieter than our first time round. I had my drip inserted next to a lady who was on her own.

'Your first try?'

'Yes. I'm so nervous.'

We felt like we could offer some reassurance to her – after all, we had had Tilo at our first attempt.

'We'll pray for you. It's all worth it in the end.'

We took the short walk from the preparation room to the theatre, hand in hand, as we prayed for our daughter. I got settled on the surgical bed, legs up and into the stirrups, confirmation of name and surname, and then the speculum to make way for the transfer.

'There she is! Our shooting star.'

The moment of seeing the flash of light as the embryo left the tube and entered the uterus was a wonder I still find difficult to describe.

'Welcome home, baby girl,' I whispered to the screen.

We left the theatre after the transfer and drove straight to a celebratory lunch to mark the birthday of one of our close friends. We were that confident. We waited out the mandatory two-week period and then went in for the blood test that would confirm the pregnancy.

'I'm sorry Mrs Tshabalala. The pregnancy was not successful.'

I couldn't believe it. I didn't want to believe it. I didn't want to have to believe it. How could it be? We had done everything by the book. What had happened? We went back to see Chris for a follow-up consultation.

'What happened?'

'The embryo did not take, unfortunately. I'm sorry. These things happen, even with IVF. We can only control so much.'

Yes, we had science, but God was the only one who could give life. I walked out of the consultation in tears, but left feeling hopeful nonetheless. Chris had that effect on you. He gave us time to work through the reasons why this transfer had not been successful but also reminded us that we still had two genetically strong embryos. We were in a more fortunate position than many couples. My body was strong, we could try again, and we could finance another round. We decided to take a two-month break to give my body a chance to recalibrate after the hormones and to focus on celebrating Tilo's first birthday and my fortieth, both in March 2024.

'You guys should not wait too long to have another one.'

'When are you falling pregnant again?'

'Should you be drinking right now? If I were you, I'd be preparing my body for another pregnancy.'

It never stopped.

It was not lost on me that my relationship with control had been completely usurped and turned on its head. If there were ever a time that I learnt that I could not control all things, this was it. I needed to surrender myself to the process and just pray that God's will would prevail. Although I had never been here before, I did realise that all of my small acts of breaking away from control had prepared me for this moment.

From the leap of faith of applying for an internship in the presidency, the outcome of which I had absolutely no control over, to the decision to follow the former deputy president into civil society instead of pursuing diplomatic service; from the blind faith of joining Tata Africa without a confirmed job, to leaving for CNBC Africa and stepping into the broadcast arena with absolutely no journalistic experience or television know-how, and then to taking the final bet on myself and leaving CNBC Africa for a path unknown – starting my own firm: The Conversation Strategists. This moment, I realised, was no different. I would have to relinquish control now too.

When my body was ready, my schedule was not.

In 2023, I'd applied for and been accepted into the International Women's Forum's (IWF) global fellowship programme. I was due to be at Harvard Business School for the last leg of the programme shortly after my birthday. We decided to delay the start of our IVF cycle until I came back because I wanted to be fully immersed in the programme without needing to administer injections throughout my time there.

Harvard had been a forever dream that I'd carried and held close to my heart and had only ever shared with my mother and Rori. I'd applied for a master's programme a few years earlier through a scholarship opportunity extended by the Centre for African Studies.

'Having had so many opportunities, why would we give you another opportunity when there are so many other people who haven't had half the chances you've had?'

The interview to get into the master's programme at Harvard a few years earlier had been tough and I had not put my best foot forward. I had not been successful. I'd called my mother and shared the outcome with her.

'Uzoya eHavanna khululeka.' You will go to Havanna, she reassured me. I corrected her multiple times that Harvard and Havanna were two very different things, but I didn't win. We carried the dream of my counting Harvard as one of the institutions I would graduate from. Now that the opportunity had arisen, I wanted to make the most of it. I proceeded to Harvard shortly after my 40th birthday and in that July we were ready to try again.

We agreed with Chris that we'd keep to the process as before, a natural cycle supported by hormonal injections and then the two-week wait. I bargained with God. If only He would grant us this, I would do this, I would do that.

'Let's recap. You have one female and one male embryo in storage. How would you like to proceed?'

Rori and I had had this conversation when we'd made the decision to try again.

'Let's go get our daughter.'

We went in again for our transfer. In our earlier visits, I'd definitely been in Camp Hope. Now I had slid all the way to Camp Desperation. This was our last girl. Drips. Stirrups. Verification. Transfer. We watched for our shooting star.

'There she is.'

I cried throughout the transfer. We had walked into, and out from, the theatre with a lot less confidence and a much deeper submission to the will of God. We appreciated science but knew that only God could give life. We went straight home and waited. Meanwhile, Tilo had now outgrown his cot and was ready to be graduated into his 'big boy' bed. We bought the bed, but the cot that he had outgrown was still in the room.

'Aunty Nozi, can we put this small bed away?' Tilo's nanny, Memory, asked as the big boy bed was being assembled.

'No, Mems. Keep it there. Our baby will come.'

I refused to dismantle the cot. Packing it away would feel like packing away my belief that we would have another baby. The cot would be for Tilo's sibling. This was my act of faith.

We had now spent a considerable amount of time at the fertility clinic. I'd become familiar with all the doctors and nurses and even the finance staff. I'd bumped into people I knew or recognised, all coming in and out of this place in hope and belief. Rori had even bumped into a family member that we'd not known was also struggling with infertility. It floored me how veiled and secretive infertility remained in our culture. We became wells of support for each other from that day on.

I was no stranger to hope and belief: of all the things I'd inherited from my parents, holding onto hope and belief was the most significant. I was raised to understand that belief was the acceptance of something as true and undeniable, and that hope was not just a feeling but a deliberate set of actions in expectation of a positive outcome. I could not have put my body through everything that IVF demanded if I didn't believe that God would give us a family. I certainly could not have done any of it if I didn't have hope that it would result in healthy children. Again, the two-week wait.

This time our two weeks were going to take us into the Christmas season. We'd bought a small plot on a rugged stretch of coastline in the Eastern Cape that formed part of the Wild Coast. With cows that roam the beach, warm waters and lush green hills, the place became a refuge for us. Time seemed to slow down and we took advantage of it and went away, quietly waiting for the call from the clinic. We spent the time walking on the beach and reflecting on everything we'd gone through. We, very intentionally, remained rooted in our gratitude for each other and for Tilo.

Two days before the anticipated call, we decided to take an early walk on the beach despite it being quite an overcast morning. Sunshine or not, we wanted to use the quiet time just to talk and, at times, also to walk in silence.

When we got back into the house, I went into the bathroom to relieve myself only to find that I was bleeding. We were losing another child. I called out for Rori. It must have been the tone in which I called for him, because I did not have the strength to project my voice in that moment, that caused him to come running to me. He saw that my face had fallen, that my tears were pooling in the crook of my collar bone. How could this be happening again? How could we be losing another child? Why was God allowing this to happen to us? Silence entered the bathroom, enveloping us. There were absolutely no words that needed to be spoken.

In my work, I coached my clients how to listen into silence to hear what it was saying. I'd point out that the iceberg model was a great illustration for understanding silence. The tip of the iceberg was what we heard in the audible realm, in the words that had been spoken. Beneath the waterline, in the silence, was a much louder conversation. In the silence we heard the fears, the dreams and even the values that kept the speaker quiet in conversation. If we could understand silence in this way, then we would hear the invitation to ask about that which sat beneath the water line.

Without words, I got up and stepped into the shower. As the water ran, Rori correctly read the signal that I needed to be alone. I heard him call the nurse to inform her of what had happened. She still wanted us to drive to the nearest lab to take the blood test anyway. So we drove away from the quiet of our rural refuge and into the city in search of a hospital where we could do the tests. The results were out in a little over an hour: we were not pregnant.

While we were in the throes of hope and heartbreak, trans-ferring and losing embryos, life was still going ahead in other spaces as if normal. I travelled to Washington for the World Bank's Annual Meetings, to Geneva to moderate a global conference on reviewing occupational health and safety stan-dards; I did a roadshow with a local client covering nine cit-ies in nine weeks and joined two boards in the course of the year. I continued to travel and work in order to meet the demands of my clients. In the throes of my deepest heart-break, my work became my refuge.

Unsurprisingly, our marriage took a knock. While I want-ed to cry out and roll up in a foetal position and scream out my pain, Rori wanted to process what was happening silently. We struggled to connect and fell silent, even with each other. We watched friends around us conceive and we cheered for them even while blinded by our own tears. With every loss, the desire for a child became all-consuming, and the pain of that longing was unbearable. Nowhere is this longing better captured than in Proverbs 30: *'There are three things that are never satisfied, four that never say, "Enough!": the grave, the barren womb, land, which is never satisfied with water, and fire, which never says, "Enough!"'*

Towards the end of 2024 we decided we'd try just one more time. We still had one male embryo that had been genetically tested and was ready for transfer. This time Chris suggested that we try a medicated cycle. This meant that my body would receive a lot more support in preparation for the transfer moment. I was put on more hormones and I was monitored more intensely. My calendar was all about working around my client commitments, my multiple scans, and check-ins. The injections stung and left my stomach with large black and blue bruises. My weight ballooned from the hormones and over a couple of weeks I piled on more than ten kilograms. More importantly, we prayed that God would give us the discipline to relinquish the control we thought we had. We had one genetically tested embryo left. Our last remaining boy. The embryo maths was all that counted at this stage: we'd started with 10 strong embryos, decided to genetically test six of the 10. Of the six tested, four were genetically strong and two were incompatible with life. From the four genetically strong eggs, we'd conceived our son, Tilo, and we'd lost both girls, and now had one male embryo that had been genetically tested left.

'Nozi, Rori, I assume we're going to transfer the last tested embryo?' Chris asked as a matter of formality.

'Actually . . . no.'

We looked at each other for reassurance of the decision we'd spoken about and made, then we looked back to him.

'We want to relinquish control. We're not going to transfer that embryo.'

'No?'

'No. We'd like to transfer any one of the four untested embryos.'

We had no idea what the chromosomal make-up of these four embryos was, but we reminded ourselves that most parents did not get to choose the sex or the chromosomal constitution of their child. Letting go of decisions felt like an act of faith. We prayed for God's will to lead the way and for us to accept the outcome of His will notwithstanding.

Drips. Stirrups. Verification. Transfer. We went back into the transfer theatre for the fourth time in two years. This time I would have to continue with the injections to the stomach and to my thighs after transfer as part of this medicated approach. The Christmas season was approaching again. We were due to receive the news of the outcome of the transfer before we left for the Wild Coast. If the news was good, this would undoubtedly be the best Christmas gift ever. If the call brought more bad news, we'd retreat into our little refuge on the Wild Coast to cry our hearts out and try to find each other through our pain.

'Mr and Mrs Tshabalala, congratulations: you're pregnant!'

I burst into tears. I had waited for this call for what seemed like forever. My body was battered and bruised from what it had gone through trying to conceive and carry another child for us both. Rori and I clung to each other and prayed in thankfulness for God's favour. God had been faithful! In a few weeks we'd have to go for our first intravaginal scan. I remembered this scan from our first pregnancy with Tilo. With the scan we'd get to hear the baby's heartbeat for the first time. I had all the expected pregnancy symptoms, and I had no reason to believe that this time would be different from when we'd first heard Tilo's heartbeat. To make it extra special, we took Tilo with us to our first scan so that he could hear the heartbeat of his brother or sister at the same time as Rori and I.

In this early stage of pregnancy, the doctor used a transducer to access the uterus intravaginally and transmit the visuals of what was happening in the uterus onto the ultrasound screen. I closed my eyes and relaxed my pelvis to make way for the device. I thought about how my body had carried us to this point. I smiled as I thought about the friendship and sibling rivalry that was about to take over our house. I thought about the cot that had patiently waited for this miracle baby to come home and share a room with Tilo.

Then I noticed the silence. My eyes fluttered to the screen. Chris kept moving the transducer, seemingly trying to get a better angle with which to see the baby. Rori held Tilo close as they both looked at the screen. The silence suffocated and ultimately delivered the bad news without anyone speaking. There was no baby! My body had done all that it was required to do. The embryo had implanted successfully but just had not grown as it was meant to. In medical terms, we had an empty gestational sac. Silence had visited us again, except this time it was in the form of an emptiness in my womb. Where our baby was meant to be was an empty sac.

I was defeated. I had no fight left. I must have stopped listening because I can't recall any of the instructions that Chris gave us about the next steps. We got home and I crawled into bed and into myself. I slept for hours with Rori keeping vigil next to me. When I awoke, he repeated the instructions from Chris. He wanted to wait a week to be certain that there was no baby. I'd have to go back for another intravaginal scan. If there was no baby, I'd have to go for a D&C the next day. A D&C is a Dilation and Curettage where the cervix is dilated and the lining of the uterus is scraped and scooped out. A D&C is typically done to get a sample of tissue in the uterus for diagnostic purposes or to clear the uterus after a miscarriage or an abortion. In our case, the procedure would clear out the gestational sac as well as the umbilical cord that had already started to form.

After the D&C procedure, we drove down to the Wild Coast to our place of refuge. I was put on strong medication to manage the pain. I drifted in and out of sleep for three days. The medication numbed my pain but left me throbbing in grief. Rori sat quietly with me when I could sit up or crawled into bed and spooned me until I fell asleep. Love pulled me from the precipice. I was at the edge of my emotional and psychological ledge. The abyss of loss and sadness yawned wide open, pulling me closer every day. I was on the verge of slipping and love brought me back. Rori's love tended me, watered me and literally kept me alive.

A few days before Christmas, friends with whom we'd scheduled time arrived and for a moment I was wrapped in their warmth. They knew the road we'd been travelling and were just the right balm for our scars. After they left, I started preparing for Christmas. I'd always grown up with Christmas being a big deal in our family. We had had one plastic Christmas tree for decades. It would come out, no matter how crooked and bent it had become over the years, and it would be decorated with the same energy, joy and vigour as the very first time. I was determined to make Christmas whole for us despite my inner fragmentation. Tilo's first Christmas had been spent with my family in Pietermaritzburg and this was the first time we'd spend the day as a nuclear family. I'd been cared for and loved through the blur of the last few weeks; I was ready to pour love into my boys too. I started the marathon cooking on Christmas eve, chopping, slicing, and dicing all the preparatory ingredients. I rose early on Christmas day to cook my specialty chicken curry, we put a leg of lamb on the braai, and accompanied our meats with an array of salads and desserts. I pulled out a box of Baker's Biscuits that had been the real treat on the Christmas menu growing up and we tucked in.

We were battered and bruised, but we were still a family, and we were still standing.

*   *   *

As we relaxed on the deck, with bellies full, slipping in and out of sleep in the late afternoon of Christmas Day, my eyes settled on the expansive sea-view in front of me. I could appreciate things in a way I couldn't before.

How many rivers had made their way here to empty out into the sea?

How different had my own journey been?

Like the meanderings of a body of water, my life had been the sum total of all the places I'd been, all the people that I'd needed to be, all the joys I'd experienced and all the pain I'd had to endure. Just as a river does not control nature's path but must find a way around the mountains and through valleys it encounters, so my life experiences had been gifts of out-of-the-box thinking, courage to find another way and the stubbornness required to follow through with action when the tough things needed to get done. While a river may be able to shape a landscape, it must also surrender to the shape of the land when the moment calls for it.

The lesson landed loudly and clearly for me: the ultimate control was the ability to flow within the world as it was, not how I wished it to be. A river ceased to be a river when it stopped moving forward. In those moments it became a pond or a dam.

My river, too, has continued to flow, carrying all the lessons and experiences of my relationship with control. In the forward movement, I cannot know what will come next. I may not always be in full control but I have and will always be in full flow.

Acknowledgements

This book is not meant to be a memoir. While it has been important for me to trace where and why I needed to be in such control, this is not a chronological account of my birth-to-death story. Rather, it is a story about releasing the need to always be in control and of coming alive to who I still can be. This is a story of a lesson learnt over too many years, a slow peeling away, layer after layer of self-discovery that has finally allowed me to begin to recalibrate my relationship with self-regulation. In these chapters you will have borne witness to my public wrestling with control. It shows up as toxic perfectionism, a crippling fear of uncertainty and a low tolerance of mistakes. I wish I could also promise that you will have read about how I've completely overcome all of these traits, but, sadly, I don't have the answers, only the lessons. And even those I'm still learning! In addition to the many conversations on my knees, and those on the therapist's couch, I've also turned to the many people whom I admire and respect and whom I have come across in my line of work as a conversation strategist. In between the interviews, the moderations and the private chats, I've received help and guidance that I didn't even know I needed. On these pages I attempt to surface these lifelines that have pulled me up, stopping me from sinking.

On the flip side of control, I'm slowly finding a firmer footing, one that allows me to show up with vulnerability and authenticity, to deepen my connection to others and to build trust that goes beyond just trusting myself. My hope is that, in sharing my story, I can extend the same lifeline to you, so that you, too, might find vulnerability, authenticity, connection and trust when you lose control.

* * *

I would not have followed through with this project had it not been for my husband and friend, Rori. He called me out every time I said, 'I don't have a story to tell,' reminding me that even the hardest pages to write might just be the healing I needed. Without Sibongile Machika, my publisher, this work would not exist: I didn't want to write a book, but in your infinite wisdom you convinced me to do so. More than anything, thank you for allowing me to break the rules and to write the book within me and not the one expected of me. Dave Gorin, thank you for being more than a sounding board, for pushing back every time I tried to hide, and for being my accountability partner who ensured that I kept every promise

I made to myself in this journey. Carol-Ann, thank you for your patience and the care with which you held my story. Without all of you, none of this would have come to pass.